ART & DESIGN

GW01043855

EDITORIAL OFFICES:
42 LEINSTER GARDENS, LONDON W2 3AN
TEL: 071-402 2141 FAX: 071-723 9540

HOUSE EDITOR: Nicola Hodges; EDITORIAL:
Katherine MacInnes; SENIOR DESIGNER:
Andrea Bettella; DESIGN CO-ORDINATOR:
Mario Bettella; DESIGN TEAM: Jacqueline
Grosvenor, Jason Rigby

SUBSCRIPTION OFFICES:
UK: VCH PUBLISHERS (UK) LTD
8 WELLINGTON COURT, WELLINGTON STREET
CAMBRIDGE CB1 1HZ UK

USA: VCH PUBLISHERS INC
303 NW 12TH AVENUE DEERFIELD BEECH,
FLORIDA 33442-1788 USA

ALL OTHER COUNTRIES:
VCH VERLAGSGESELLSCHAFT MBH
BOSCHSTRASSE 12, POSTFACH 101161
69451 WEINHEIM GERMANY

CONTENTS

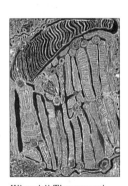

River Run, *choreography Laurie Booth, stage set Anish Kapoor, London, 1993*

ACHILLE BONITO OLIVA
INTERVIEW WITH GABRIELLA DALESIO

In this Art & Design *interview Achille Bonito Oliva talks to Rome-based art critic Gabriella Dalesio about the intellectual adventure he has embarked on in directing the 45th Venice Biennale, which he has called the 'Cardinal Points of Art'. He discusses the Biennale's emphasis on the themes of nomadism and multiculturalism and also elucidates his own highly idiosyncratic style of art criticism.*

Gabriella Dalesio: *You have been on the art scene since 1967, when you joined Gruppo '63. One of the most noticeable characteristics that distinguishes you from other critics and historians of your generation is your curiosity, your desire to understand all that is contemporary. What is it that moves you in your intensely personal and conflicting encounter with art?*

Achille Bonito Oliva: Well, I believe that at the bottom of it all there's an intellectual adventure that has as its impetus a sort of self-regeneration of the motivation itself; in the sense that I always and systematically move following a style that is concerned with an internal and external conflict.

This play of balances, which is also psychological, is able to get round any geometry of coherence and of linear development; but this does not necessarily imply a strategy of transgression. I don't believe so much in transgression as I do in the sense of play typical of the Neapolitan outlook. This is best represented by the modern Socrates, Toto [post-war Neapolitan popular comedian], who, all considered, had his comedy 'ready-made' in his catch phrase 'a prescindere' [loosely translated as 'everything considered and besides']. I would say that 'a prescindere' is somewhat the emblem of my cultural exploits.

– The 'Cardinal Points Of Art', the Biennale you have organised, echoes in its multi-disciplined complexity another project you undertook in 1973 which marked the exhibition history of the last 20 years: I'm referring to the international exhibition 'Contemporanea'. You had at that time already talked about the laterality of the critical gaze, of the role and the power of the critic concerning the admission of art in the art system. What is it that distinguishes this coherence after so many years?

What distinguishes it, to begin with, is the change of scale of the project; in the sense that now I have

somehow produced a great exhibitive enterprise which is also a form of exhibitive scripture. Through directing this exhibition I've moved today from the role of designer of criticism to that of architect of criticism, of someone who can lay out an installation and a complex construction which utilises many working groups, but all sustained by a plan laid out by myself.

The difference between 'Contemporanea' and 'Cardinal Points Of Art' lies within the fact that in the former I staged an inter-disciplinary exhibition stemming from a historical exposition that went backwards from 1973 to 1955. Now, on the other hand, 'Cardinal Points Of Art' tends to be a project – and in this respect I'm talking about architecture of criticism – that dwells not only in the specifics of art, but also in the culture of political and theoretical thinking. I mean that the 'Cardinal Points Of Art' aspire to present themselves as a reading of a widened, no longer strictly Western, historical context. This is no longer played on the old frontiers of American/European internationalism – frontal dialectics that in 1973 were in their prime and were then well represented with 'Contemporanea' through a balanced measure of 45 European artists and 45 Americans. Instead after the purging action of post-modern culture and the trans-avant-garde – that have somehow opened frontiers, which I would call lateral, blowing up the linguistic Darwinism of the neo-avantgardes and breaking the linearity of evolution of post-war art – we have now moved to a widening of new frontiers of internationalism stretched across an inter-continental geography.

It is in this sense that this theoretical dome works, founded on the astrophysical concept of the cardinal points (of art): North, South, East, West. In other words, there is a circularity of languages, cultures, ideas that, after the recently deposed bi-polarity of the beginning of the second half of the century – North-South first, leaning towards primitive cultures and then East-West and, conversely, leaning towards the East – offers the possibility for the artist and for the public to perform a 360 degree turn and observe other cultures.

– In your introductory essay to this Biennale you touch a few issues that affect, today, the planetary daily life; the transitionality, the nomadism, the fragmentation which are characteristics of a new Babylon and of a new technological middle age, which we witness in a syn-aesthetic manner. Don't

OPPOSITE: View of Venice, video still by Raymond O'Daly

you think this requires more than a sociological assessment, or in this case, as you call it, astrophysical, and how does it fit with the new theories of complexity?

I think this exhibition is really the expression of the theory of complexity, or rather of the sets theory. It is really the proposal for a project that plays on a mosaic structure, in which every tile develops a thematic exhibition, either on a context or a monograph, avoiding the homologation that existed in great exhibitions like Kassel or 'Les Magiciens de la Terre'. In the first one it took place under the Germany-United States axis, in the second under the blows of a colonialist paternalism that tried to marry Western artistic research to third world crafts. This doesn't happen in this case because by actually utilising the theory of sets there somehow is a respect for complexity and also a specificity through exhibitions on Western research with 16 examples of points of art.

'Passage To The East', for example, re-introduces groups like the Lettristi and the Gutai onto the great international exhibitions scene. These groups were always marginalised and removed from the international cultural conscience for being predecessors of many movements which eventually appeared in the 60s, 70s, and 80s, up to the young Chinese painters, bearers of a very personal iconography of conceptual realism, which does not develop an ideologist image of those cultures, but one that is utterly parallel to what is produced in the West, even if completely comparable.

– The message that really emerges from the 'Aperto' section, inspired by the post-human invention of the financier-critic Jeffrey Deitch is one of death and necrophilia. Don't you think that the message of art is one of life and the opening of new frontiers, rather than the acceptance of rules, fashions, tendencies administered and decided by international financial capital?

Even if there is a section in the care of Jeffrey Deitch, this doesn't mean that 'Aperto 93' is inspired by this, if anything because the 'Aperto' project is signed by me personally. After 1980, when I invented 'Aperto' – which received its baptism in its first edition through the exhibition of the hot phase of the international trans-avantgarde – I conclude the journey in 1993 by exhibiting the cold trans-avantgarde denoted by a linguistic strategy that even now belongs to the culture of post-modernism, in other words the destructuralisation, the assembling, the re-conversion, the contamination. These were all operative concepts in the 80s, even if then they were used in the classical genres of painting and sculpture, they are now applied to a subject matter that does possess, a terribleness, but that is not completely comparable, if you'll allow me, to the post-human of which Deitch speaks. I also believe that in this instance

there is a progression from the neutrality that post-humanism gives you. There is instead an orientation, readily given in the title 'Emergency', to invite those artists that work on the five emergencies: violence, entropy, difference, marginalisation and survival. The intention is to emphasise, somehow, the determination of the new generation that is far removed from the generation of the 50s although it had the same notion of determination, because today it filters it through language, research or the citation of avantgarde languages. This sort of aestheticism of which you speak . . .

– Aestheticism of the horrific . . .

This is the effect of a cultural anthropology typical of this decade.

– It seems to me that this is more a sociological ascertaining than an indication . . .

Art never gives recipes. You must understand that an exhibition is the planning of an investigation on the world, a request for an inquest on things, never a precept or an answer. In this instance too, the images of 'Aperto' are like iconographical stations that come to document a universe which is the one we live in.

– A part of it.

I would say that 'Aperto' is a single work. You must believe that these really are all exhibitions set to realise a project of mine with a mosaic structure. I see 'Aperto' as the configuration of an exhibition articulated in various passages.

– This Biennale comes to light under the banner of an Italy bravely reviewing its faults, dating back 40 years, but also under the sign of a big political and institutional crisis. How do you see the possibility of survival for this almost centennial exhibition?

I not only see it, but I've demonstrated it to be possible with a strong project in a weak situation and which has an international solidarity, managing to bring to Venice a cosmopolitan world which didn't happen even at Kassel; managing to bring to Venice events, situations, atmospheres that, in the words of Leo Castelli and Ileana Sonnabend, have not been seen in Venice since 1948.

This is the result of an idea, a critical conduction and coherence on my behalf which has brought me to put my name to a project pluralistically calling to it a series of Italian and foreign collaborators who have each brought their specific expertise. Even in this circumstance the project is assured its exactness and precision. In other words, I've worked constantly monitoring the project, or, to put it another way, pragmatically refining it moment by moment until the end, through a progressive method of attention and control, without any projectual self-conceit, in fact giving the project that flexibility capable of finding its definition at its inauguration.

– In your splendid text 'Magic Territory' you asserted that 'The terrible has already happened' and you wrote: 'The birth of the artist finds a world already highly articulated and a fall of humanity in the area of affirmation of principles. The process of technological development is so advanced that it implies a loss of concreteness in the world and a reduction of the possibilities of the imagination'. You still believed then in the tactical dislocations of the artist in his own fantasy, as a symptom of existential fluidity.

Do you think that this existential anarchy is still possible regarding papier-mâché scenarios marked by the real life dramas of daily conflicts?

I will answer you as did Ernest Junger at the press conference here in Venice when I gave him the 'Cardinal Points Of Art' Prize. To begin with, Junger, who is a pure writer who resides at the alpine heights of the purity of Friedrich, didn't find this Biennale a papier-mâché universe, in fact . . .

– But I've never said that.

I'd like to tell you more, again citing Junger, who preferred Hölderlin to Hegel's death of art, in other words a tautological necessity for art and poetry to confirm themselves at any time and beyond any coherence. As far as I'm concerned, I've always refused the dialectic principle and I've confirmed through my work the principle of contradiction.

– In fact, I was talking about anarchy . . .

As regards anarchy, in this Biennale I waver between two figures, the Marco Polo and the Casanova. In fact, in my new book *Conversation Please*, published now by Alemanni, I allow myself to hold conversations with various figures, Medardo Rosso, Giulio Romano, Duchamp, Walter Benjamin and my ancestor Giuseppe Bonito, a well known 18th-century painter at the Bourbon Court in Naples. Therefore a Casanova of knowledge, a Don Juan of knowledge, someone who develops a project with progressing stations, with pauses at both pleasure and knowledge, but also a Marco Polo, as someone who draws itineraries establishing a geography of paths capable of reducing and contracting distances. Out of this then comes 'Passage to the East', the John Cage exhibition, and a marriage and a presentation of diverse artists.

There is then, in this respect, the confirmation of the cultural anthropology of a city like Venice, which should name Marco Polo not only its airport but Piazza San Marco as well. Because Piazza San Marco itself is the institution of a space, an installation of sorts, the fruit of a spatial geometry and architectural contamination. It really is the conformation and the shell of the culture that is travel.

I maintain that from 'Magic Territory' to the Trans-Avantgarde I developed a concept of cultural nomadism that has now transformed itself into social nomadism through the massive migrations of the Eastern populations to the West and that have changed the concept of nationality, sometimes rather dramatically. I introduce this concept of nomadism in the project but I think that in the 90s it can't be confronted in hedonistic terms, but by finding again a sense of direction that has the cardinal points of art as reference.

From here then, Marco Polo and a project finalised and set to describe a reality in which every exhibition is an image and a segment of a project that as a whole is all set to propose in scale an expositive graphology that allows me today to confirm myself as architect of art criticism.

– The enjoyable and arduous adventure of preparing this Biennale has seen you roaming from China to Tibet, from Africa to Australia, and other remote places in the world. What kind of influence has this experience had on your vision as an art critic, and how?

To me it signified a travel rapport, a process of expanded wisdom, a capillary capacity for knowledge that in reality I had only suspected. It also meant the unwinding of my curiosity through tangible situations of contact and rapport. It meant a personal and solid intellectual adventure.
(Translated by Paolo Valli)

A

B

C

VI

D

THE UNCLE MIKEY FINE ART GAMESHOW
VENICE BIENNALE 1993
By Michael Petry

The following real life story from the Venice Biennale illustrates in words and images how Uncle Mikey (artist Michael Petry), eversmiling, managed to make the best of a raw deal making friends as he went.

The Uncle Mikey Fine Art Gameshow was part of the official Biennale programme, as part of the Casino Container at the Riva dei Sette Martiri. The Container was to have been a global network station linking artists around the world with Venice and the Biennale. Unfortunately it didn't. Through the Machiavellian machinations of the Commune of Venice (the city government) the Container was held to ransom on the day it was to be erected. A mysterious and previously undiscussed 'rental' of 20,000,000 lire was to be handed over (preferably in used notes) to a certain city official. A Sra Miralia also proved to be a stumbling block as it was her job to sign an official document stating that all the city permits were in order (as indeed they were). No, thanks to the Technical Director of the Biennale, Bruno Seggi leaving this to the Container's organisers as he had a conflict of interest concerning his wife, Uncle Mikey and 40 artists from around the world arrived to find they had no building to do their projects in, and everything in one big mess.

Uncle Mikey, the ultimate American gameshow host, who spoke no foreign languages, arrived with his camera crew and decided on the spot to become an investigative reporter, to root out corruption, to go to the streets, city hall, and the gardens of the Biennale to cover the event, since the show must go on. The eversmiling, overly friendly, Uncle Mikey kept reminding his fellow artists of his famous catchphrase 'Smile, it's ART!!!' since the only alternative was tears.

Life intervened to imitate art. The official theme of the Biennale was Emergency, and that is where the Container Project, its organisers Reinhard Muller, Meyer and Sabine Voggenreiter, Uwe Wagner and Axel Wirths, and the artists (from as far away as Japan, Australia, and the USA) found themselves. The Gameshow was to have been one of the *in situ* works, and was to have been a satire on the current art world and international media manipulation of art and ideas. The Gameshow was to have linked up with live radio call in programmes in Britain, the USA, and Germany. The audience would have been given the opportunity to answer questions on the art world, with real art works as prizes. Uncle Mikey's overtly facile treatment of Art, to the point of excluding it, would have focused on the media's notion of Art, by its obvious absence.

The Gameshow may still go ahead, as Uncle Mikey has successfully solicited art prizes from artists around the world. Robert Longo, Louise Lawler, Sylvie Fluery, Mike Bidlo, Lilliane Lijn, Colette Richmond Burton, Antonio Musella, Lam de Wolf, Joni Mabe, Ultraviolet, Tatsuo Miyajima and Jasper Johns were amongst the many artists who kindly gave a prize. Uncle Mikey may still go ahead, but Coca Cola, the main Container sponsor, has pulled out. The situation in Venice has deteriorated to such an extent, that the Mayor and all his cronies have been removed by dictat from Rome, and the city is currently being run by a central government commissioner.

Without a building to transmit from, Uncle Mikey interviewed artists, gallerists and curators and they are pictured here. The *Uncle Mikey Themetune* by John Powell is available on cassette. And for a limited time only, readers of *A&D* can have their very own Uncle Mikey Smile Badge – FREE! All you need to do to receive your signed Badge is send your name and address to *A&D* Supplies, 42 Leinster Gardens, London W2 3AN. Offer good while stocks last. Send today to avoid disappointment.
(Cameraman: Raymond O'Daly)

BACKGROUND: Uncle Mikey and the 'Hermaphrodite Twins in Art' Adela and Eva from Germany *A* Uncle Mikey says 'Hi' from the Giardini *B* Holly Solomon sends a kiss to her sons *C* Uncle Mikey with Yayoi Kusama, the artist for the Japanese Pavilion *D* James Lee Byars, 'The Fabulous Jill' and Uncle Mikey in the Benetton Room at the Aperto *OVERLEAF BACKGROUND:* Japanese Pavilion *E* Uncle Mikey touches the Gabriel Orozco *F* The Slovenian Cultural Attache explains art to Uncle Mikey *G* Stuart Morgan and Uncle Mikey *H* Uncle Mikey in the German Pavilion with the Hans Haacke Installation *I* Sra Miralia (Venice City Councillor) denies all knowledge of everything to Uncle Mikey *J* Uncle Mikey and the World Flag Art Farm by Yuki Nori Yan Agi (Animal Rights protestors forced the Biennale to free the ants) *K* Uncle Mikey touches a Louise Bourgeois Rubber Sculpture at the American Pavilion

E

F

G

H

GERMANIA

I

J

K

IX

BOOKS

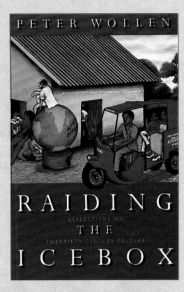

RAIDING THE ICEBOX – Reflections on 20th-Century Culture by Peter Wollen, Verso, London, 1993, 222pp, HB £34.95/ PB £10.95
Beginning with an analysis of the role of Diaghilev and the Russian Ballet, Wollen argues that Modernism has always had a hidden suppressed side which cannot easily be absorbed into the master-narrative of modernity. He suggests, through reconsiderations of Matisse's Moroccan paintings and the work of the great fashion designer Paul Poiret, that the history of high art cannot be written separately from that of performance and design. Wollen goes on to review the hopes, fears and expectations of artists and critics fascinated by Henry Ford's assembly line as much as by the Hollywood dream factory, concluding with Guy Debord's caustic dystopian vision of an all-consuming 'Society of the Spectacle'. He chronicles the emergence of a subversive new sensibility in the underground films of Andy Warhol, and explores some of the cultural forms which non-Western artists are using as modernism enters into crisis and the century draws to a close raiding the icebox of the West.

AZTEC ART by Esther Pasztory, Abrams, London, 1993, 336pp, b/w and colour ills, HB £40.
In the popular view, Aztec culture represents the ultimate in human cruelty and bloodthirstiness, and its art is the macabre expression and illustration of this culture. The Aztec sense of philosophical inquiry, poetry, and cosmic vision present an altogether different impression of austere priests who humbly carried out their hard pact with the supernatural. Aztec Art is either dismissed as grotesque and primitive or exalted as a religious vision. It is rarely studied with the objectivity accorded to the art of most civilisations. Although their culture had been in existence only a few hundred years prior to the 16th-century Spanish conquest of Mexico, majestic stone sculptures carved without metal tools, lost techniques of featherwork and turquoise mosaic, painted books and intricate and symbolic temple architecture are evidence of their culture and art.

Dr Esther Pasztory combines her knowledge of archaeological research and Aztec art to guide the reader through the maze of material. By providing parallels between artistic traits and contemporary socio-historical events she allows a full and clear and academic understanding of the period.

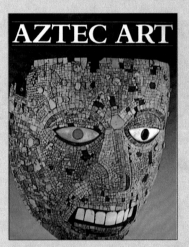

AFFIRMATIONS AND REFUSALS, The collected essays and criticism of Clement Greenberg, Volume 3, edited by John O' Brian, University of Chicago Press, London, 1993, 305pp, HB
'Anything in art that is surprising enough to be puzzling usually causes discomfort. It depends on the critic's sincerity whether he will suspend judgement and endure the discomfort until he is no longer puzzled. Often, however, he is tempted to ease himself by immediately pronouncing 'bad'.' This is taken from a section entitled, 'The European View of American Art' – dangerous words from such an influential critic. Greenberg is widely recognised as the most articulate champion of modernism during its American ascendancy after World War II. This collection of his articles is introduced by him and includes a brief summary of events that places the criticism in its artistic and historical context. Volume 4 of this collection, also edited by John O' Brian is called *Modernism with a Vengeance*.

HISTORY OF JAPANESE ART by Penelope Mason, Abrams, 1993, 431pp, b/w and colour ills, HB £45. Penelope Mason treats Japanese arts as an expression of the countries social and religious traditions to produce an insight into the Japanese mind – a subject which fascinates Western thinkers. This is a comprehensive examination of the painting, sculpture, architecture and ceramics of Japan from prehistoric times to the outbreak of the Second World War.

The reader is encouraged to pause and look at the works in depth – from the 7th-century Horyuji temple complex near Nara to an early 12th-century hand scroll illustrating the 'Tale of Genji' to a glazed 19th-century tea-ceremony vessel. The fluid economy of their painting technique can be applied with equal effect to express the terrifying determination of their warriors or the languid modesty of Japanese etiquette. Artistic even in their written figures the Japanese have a unique sensitivity to art evident in their intricate, asymmetrical landscape designs.

From an art historical point of view, since the economy of Whistler's Japonism, we have only just begun to appreciate the sophistication of the abstract nature of Japanese art. Works such as the 12th-century cover of Chapter 27 of *Heike nokyo*, serve to remind us that a slavish attention to realistic detail hampered British art until the turn of this century.

BOOKS RECEIVED:

WHY FAKES MATTER, Essays on Problems of Authenticity *edited by Mark Jones, British Museum Press, London, 1992, 198pp, b/w ills, HB £35*

THE PRINT IN GERMANY 1880-1933 The Age of Expressionism *by Frances Carey and Antony Griffiths, British Museums Press, London, 272pp, b/w and colour ills PB £16.95*

EXPLORATION IN WOOD, The Furniture & Sculpture of Tim Stead *by Giles Sutherland, Canongate Press, Edinburgh, 1993, 100pp, colour ills, HB £25*

MAK Austrian Museum of Applied Arts, *edited by Peter Noever, Prestel Museum Guide, 144pp, colour ills, PB*

SILENT ENERGY *edited by David Elliot and Lydie Mepham, The Museum of Modern Art, Oxford, 1993, 24pp, b/w and colour ills, PB*

ROGER ACKLING, *Centre d'Art Contemporain Genéve in association with Annely Juda Fine Art, London, 1993, 20pp, colour ills, PB*

HAMISH FULTON, Only art resulting from the experience of individual walks, *Annely Juda Fine Art, 1993, 20pp, b/w ills, PB*

THE FLY WITH THE WINGS *by Ilya Kabakov, Abrams, Four Volumes 1993, 244pp, colour ills, PB £65*

MENTAL INSTITUTION OR INSTITUTE OF CREATIVE RESEARCH *by Ilya Kabakov, Abrams, 1993, 248pp, colour ills, PB £65*

HE DANCER AND THE DANCE: Merce Cunningham in Conversation with Jacqueline Lesschaeve, *Marion Boyars, London, 1991, 238 pp, b/w ills, PB £12.95.*

ARTISTS AT GEMINI G.E.L, *Celebrating the 25th Year by Mark Rosenthal, Abrams, 1993, 208pp, colour ills, PB £45*

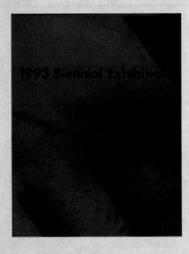

1993 BIENNIAL EXHIBITION
Whitney Museum of American Art, New York, 1993, 288pp, PB
This catalogue presents essays by a wide range of respected contemporary art historians. Homi K Bhabha writes on 'Beyond the Pale: Art in the Age of Multicultural Translation' in which he analyses 'the beyond' which is: 'neither a new horizon nor a leaving behind of the past . . . Beginnings and endings may be the sustaining myths of the middle years: but in the *fin de siècle*, we find ourselves in the moment of transit where space and time cross to produce complex figures of difference and identity, past and present, inside and outside, inclusion and exclusion.' Coco Fusco's essay on 'Passionate Irreverence: The Cultural Politics of Identity' concludes that to build on the collective memories of our vision of America, we must draw on those storehouses of identity which once activated become power sites of cultural resistance. The artists are presented with their CVs, list of exhibitions and a bibliography. The exhibits range from La Cama a garishly decorated four poster complete with icon-like sun head board by Pepon Osorio to the brutal frescos of Suzanne McClelland.

DANCE AS TEXT, Ideologies of the Baroque Body
by Mark Franko, Cambridge University Press, Cambridge, 1993, 237pp, HB £40
This book provides a picture of the complex theoretical underpinnings of composite spectacle, the ideological tensions underlying experiments with autonomous dance, and finally, the subversiveness of Moliére's use of court ballet traditions. This historical and theoretical examination of French court ballet spans a hundred-year period, beginning in 1573 touching on the late Renaissance and the early Baroque. Utilising aesthetic and ideological criteria, Mark Franko analyses court ballet librettos, contemporary performance theory, and related commentary on dance and movement in the literature of this period. Examining the formal choreographic apparatus that characterises late Valois and early Bourbon ballet spectacle, Franko postulates that the evolving aesthetic ultimately reflected the political situation of the noble class, which devised and performed court ballets. He shows how the body emerged from verbal theatre as a self-sufficient text whose autonomy had varied ideological connotations, most important among which was the expression of noble resistance to the increasingly absolutist monarchy. Franko's analysis blends archival research with critical and cultural theory in order to resituate the burlesque tradition in its politically volatile context.

LETTERS FROM THE PEOPLE
by Lee Friedlander, Jonathan Cape, 1993, 214pp, HB £75.
Beginning with individual letters of the alphabet, found as graffiti or as part of street signs, shop windows, vehicle graphics or advertising hoardings, he moves into numerals, and then into whole sentences. Far from being a simple alphabet, the work addresses the roots of language itself, building into a great epic poem, resonant with the voices of the street. Friedlander is a photographer in the tradition of Walker Evans, whose book *Message from the Interior*, provided the scale on which this book is based. Graffiti is visual communication in its rawest sense. Words in neon, words in paint – dripping, numbers in sturdy enamel and in hastily scribbled chalk – these all express the immediacy of our time.

DRAWING THE LINE Art and Cultural Identity in Contemporary Latin America
by Oriana Baddeley and Valerie Fraser, Verso, 1993, 164pp, PB £11.95
Recent international interest in painters such as Kahlo, Rivera and Orozco has brought Latin American art to a wider audience than ever before but failed to confront its continuing marginalisation within art criticism. This explores the areas occupied by Latin American art and culture between the ongoing traditions of the subcontinent's indigenous inhabitants, its colonial heritage and its contemporary relationship to the cultural politics of North America and Europe. The book looks at the frequent subversion of dominant images and conventions of European art – such as the political significance of landscape painting or the constant reworking of familiar icons of European art – and explores the significance of popular art – such as the Chilean arpilleras which commemorate the 'disappeared' of Pinochet's regime –relating them to the traditional 'high/low art' dichotomy.

RICHARD HAMILTON
The Venice Biennale, British Pavilion, with texts by Sarat Maharaj, British Council, 40pp, colour ills, PB
Designed like a glossy culture magazine with sections such as 'News from Abroad', 'Arts and Entertainment', 'Health and Beauty' – Hamilton uses his art to parody conventional journalism. However, unlike those journalists his artistic stance allows him to tackle in a clearsighted way controversial issues such as Northern Ireland and the Gulf.

EXHIBITIONS

ARATJARA – Art of the First Australians

The most extraordinary phenomenon of Aboriginal Art is its relationship to time – although it is the oldest art in the world it is also current, up-to-date and the most genuine representation of the present Australian cultural paradox. The conventional ritual design of gods uses thick dark lines dotted with white to represent the power of the ancestral beings invoked. This technique is abstracted in contemporary art to produce kinetic works which resonate while at the same time revealing their traditional organic and even visceral roots.

More figurative work such as Les Midikuria's *Petrol Sniffer* 1988 represents a socio-political problem that has been interpreted using traditional art techniques. However, the symbolism found in more abstract works is less obvious. *The 'Rainbow Serpent at Pikilli'* 1989 by 'Pansy Napangati, is a 'Dreamtime' ancestor spirit often depicted swallowing people whom it later regurgitates in a transformed state as features of the landscape. This action is often used in Aboriginal art as a metaphor for the transition from one metaphysical state of being into another. The events of the Dreaming provide the great themes of Aboriginal art. The concept of 'dreaming' does not refer to the state of dreams or unreality but rather to a reality beyond the mundane providing a framework by which human society retains a harmonious equilibrium with the universe.

Hayward Gallery, London, 23 July to 10 October 1993

CHINA TRANSFORMED – New Art From China

Since the events of June 1989, there has been little official tolerance of avant-garde values but, a gradual process of normalisation has taken place and 1993 marks a year of increasing exposure of Chinese contemporary art. 'China Transformed' is an exhibition in two parts dedicated to the spirit and achievement of a new generation of artists who emerged in China in the mid 80s. After decades of seclusion from the art of the West under Communism and the Cold War, young Chinese artists have used a new-found awareness of the wider world to confront their history and tradition producing works of great originality and dynamism. In 'Silent Energy' specially commissioned works highlight the different perspectives of East and West by making social, political, ecological and art-historical references. The 'Chinese Avant-Garde' tackles two broad tendencies: one of technical innovation and the search for new for... guages and the other ... ... of the ideologie... ... the dominant c...

...artist... ...s of this exhibitio...

...Art ...
...
Chin...

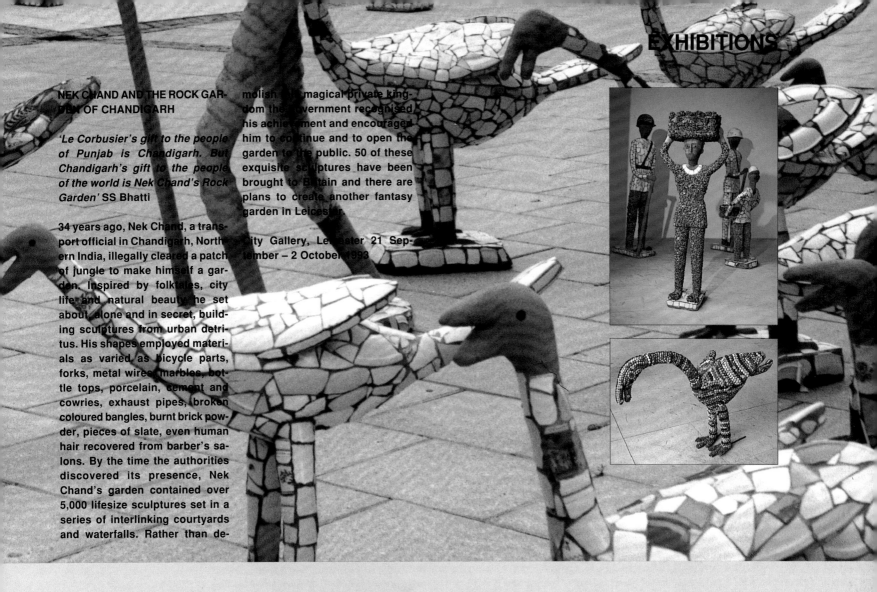

NEK CHAND AND THE ROCK GARDEN OF CHANDIGARH

'Le Corbusier's gift to the people of Punjab is Chandigarh. But Chandigarh's gift to the people of the world is Nek Chand's Rock Garden' SS Bhatti

34 years ago, Nek Chand, a transport official in Chandigarh, Northern India, illegally cleared a patch of jungle to make himself a garden. Inspired by folktales, city life and natural beauty he set about, alone and in secret, building sculptures from urban detritus. His shapes employed materials as varied as bicycle parts, forks, metal wires, marbles, bottle tops, porcelain, cement and cowries, exhaust pipes, broken coloured bangles, burnt brick powder, pieces of slate, even human hair recovered from barber's salons. By the time the authorities discovered its presence, Nek Chand's garden contained over 5,000 lifesize sculptures set in a series of interlinking courtyards and waterfalls. Rather than de-

molish this magical private kingdom the government recognised his achievement and encouraged him to continue and to open the garden to the public. 50 of these exquisite sculptures have been brought to Britain and there are plans to create another fantasy garden in Leicester.

City Gallery, Leicester 21 September – 2 October 1993

OAXACA, MAGIC OF MEXICO

This is only the second occasion that the Europalia Biennial has invited a non-European country to present its cultural achievements. The 1993 show concentrates on the State of Oaxaca, an area south of Mexico City and west of Yucatán where the Zapotec and Mixtec cultures flourished from 1500-900 AD. A chronological survey follows the course of Mexican culture from the pre-Columbian through the Colonial period to the present day.

Much of the Zapotec work comes from the city of Monte Albán – objects such as calendars and hieroglyphic and mathematical inscriptions describe a high level of scientific knowledge and advanced technical and artistic skills are revealed through polychrome ceramics, burial urns and jewellery in gold and jade. The Zapotecs were displaced by the Mixtecs at the beginning of the second millennium and Monte Albán was turned into a necropolis where Mixtecan dignitaries

were buried with elaborately worked intricate offerings in gold and silver. As a Vice-Regal centre in the 16th-18th century the colonial art of Oaxaca was very rich. Evidence of the missionary zeal of the first settlers can be seen in religous artifacts discovered in Dominican convents. The work of contemporary artists such as Rufino Tamayo, Francisco Toledo and Rodolfo Nieto combines a deep understanding of this rich cultural history with the present social and political context.

Part of the Europalia 93 Festival in the Netherlands, 23 September – 19 December 1993

MUSEUMS

TATE GALLERY, St Ives, Cornwall

The creation in 1980 of the Barbara Hepworth museum, managed by the Trustees of the Tate Gallery, was prompted by her request to consider 'the practicality of establishing a permanent exhibition of some of my works in Trewyn studio and its garden'. It was unique in this country in presenting the artist's work in the environment in which she lived and worked. The Tate Gallery, St Ives seeks to achieve the same aim on a larger scale. It was designed by the architects Eldred Evans and David Shalev, to show the Tate's pre-eminent collection of works by 20th-century St Ives artists, in the surroundings and atmosphere in which they were created. The gallery is a three-storey building backing directly into the cliff face, exploiting the dramatic sea views offered by the site. It is comprised of studio-like daylit rooms arranged in a simple sequence around a secret courtyard entered through a small amphitheatre space which forms a window onto the Atlantic. In creating spaces of varying shape, size and quantity of light, the intention was to highlight the paintings and objects and create a relaxed atmosphere highly conducive to experiencing the art.

Many artists are associated with St Ives and West Cornwall its rich history and its vivid artistic life. Ben Nicholson and Christopher Wood were the first to find inspiration here, they met Alfred Wallis the retired seaman whose naive art had a profound influence on their work. *The Times* Arts reporter, Alison Roberts Graham Morris, café owner and member of the St Ives Chamber of Trade committee remembers Wallis paying his bill at the bakery in paintings. 'Every Monday morning, the baker would start his fire with one or two of the pictures – he didn't think they were much good and Alfred Wallis always said he only painted to please himself'. Ben Nicholson, Barbara Hepworth and Naum Gabo settled here in 1939

establishing an outpost for the abstract avant-garde. The potters Bernard Leach and Shoji Hamada established an internationally recognised ceramic movement from St Ives. After the war, a younger generation including Wilhelmina Barns-Graham, Peter Lanyon, John Wells, Denis Mitchell, Paul Feiler, Terry Frost, Bryan Wynter, Patrick Heron and Roger Hilton emerged.

A large coloured glass window, shown here, dominates the gallery's entrance area. It was specially designed by Patrick Heron. Its fabrication called for an innovative lamination technique which allows the colours in the stained glass to join without traditional leading.

REOPENING OF MAK – Austrian Museum of Applied Arts, Vienna

'If a museum of art does not constantly pursue a course of critical confrontation with the arts, does not recognise contemporary art's modes of perception and viewpoints as a challenge to reassess its own position, it deprives itself of its very raison d'etre. The idea of 'preserving' objects and the elements that constitute a collection is inseparably linked to the responsibility to demonstrate and make visible their contemporary relevance.' Peter Noever Director, MAK

With this in mind MAK has undergone a massive restructuring the results of which were seen at the recent reopening entitled 'Between Tradition and Experiment'. One distinctive feature of this scheme was the invitation of internationally renowned artists to help redesign the displays of the museum's collections placing them within a contemporary context and in some cases develping entirely new spatial concepts. Amongst these Günther Förg helped design the Romanesque Gothic Renaissance collection; Donald Judd the Baroque Rococo Classicism, Jenny Holzer the Empire Style Biedermeier; Barbara Bloom the Historicism Art Nouveau and GANG ART the Oriental.

MAK has also commissioned specially created art works including works by Magdalena Jetelová, Walter Pichler, Bernard Rudofsky and Vito Acconci whose installation *The City Inside Us* (*BACKGROUND*) was shown between March and August 1993.

ABOVE: Romanesque Gothic Renaissance, designing artist Günther Förg, display cases Matthias Esterhazy, curator Angela Völker '. . . a connection had to be made between the delicate colouring of the Göss paraments, the strong, unfaded colours of the majolica, here dominantly ultramarine and ochre, and the room's ceiling colour. I decided on a light cobalt blue, which has a certain festive quality, but is also discordant with the colour of the ceiling'; *BELOW*: Empire Style Biedermeier, designing artist Jenny Holzer, curator Christian Witt-Dörring '. . . I wanted to find another system to present information about the collection and about the times in which the objects were made . . . I chose electronic signs with large memories to talk about why what was produced and for whom . . . I also rearranged the furniture, silverware, glassware, and porcelain, as would any good housewife.'

THE BODY

Journal of Philosophy & the Visual Arts No 4
Edited by Andrew Benjamin

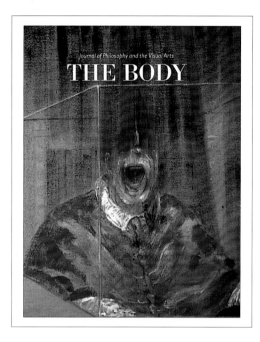

'. . . and often I have asked myself whether, taking a large view, philosophy has not been merely an interpretation of the body and a misunderstanding of the body.' Nietzsche

Whether there is a sense of being contained or trapped in a body, or of viewing it from the outside, these emotions are frequently externalised in creativity. This issue deals incisively with the reaction, as a woman, to the idea of being 'contained' by the body; with the delicate distinction between the homosexual and the homoerotic; with the physical effects of paintings on the body, exemplified by Francis **Bacon**'s use of 'violence of sensations'; with gender in art based on the ideology of the society in which **Degas** as painter created his work; with the effect of Thomas **Eakins**' male nudes on late nineteenth-century American society; and with the dependence of the concept of architecture on the model of a unified body.

A section representing contemporary artists includes Michael **Petry**'s *Chemistry of Love*; Helen **Chadwick**'s *Piss Flowers*; Kiki **Smith**'s flayed frames, Daniel **Kurjakovic** on Louise **Sudell** and Matthew **Barney**'s violently erotic images. Along with contributions from Greg **Lynn**, Mark **Rakatansky**, Christine **Battersby** and Parveen **Adams**, this issue of the *Journal of Philosophy & the Visual Arts* covers in detail the question of art and the human body: the sexual, the political and the physical.

ISBN: 1 85490 212 1 £14.95 PB
278 x 222 mm, 96 pages in full colour
Publication: October

ACADEMY GROUP LTD

42 LEINSTER GARDENS, LONDON W2 3AN TEL: 071-402 2141 FAX: 071-723 9540
TRADE ORDERS: VCH, 8 WELLINGTON COURT, WELLINGTON STREET, CAMBRIDGE, CB1 1HZ TEL: 0223 321111 FAX: 0223 313321

PARALLEL STRUCTURES

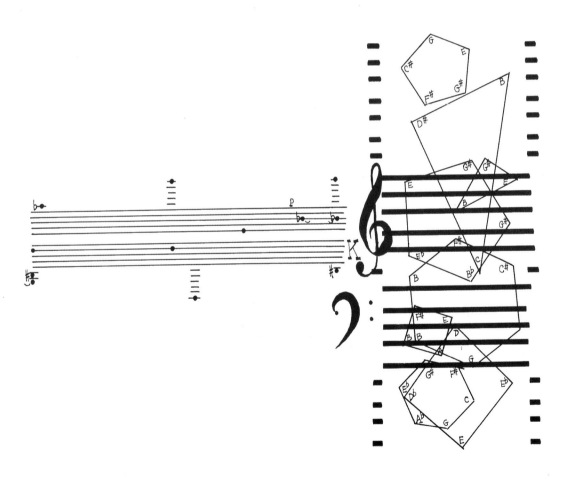

John Cage, 'Solo for Piano', page 8 (detail), from Concert for Piano and Orchestra, *1957-58, 63 pages, ink on paper, each page 28 x 42.8 cm, Northwestern University Music Library, John Cage 'Notations' Collection, photo Prudence Cuming Associates*

Art & Design

PARALLEL STRUCTURES
A R T D A N C E M U S I C

ABOVE: Val Wilmer, Richard Davis, *New York, 1967;*
OPPOSITE: Anish Kapoor, Eyes Turned Inward *(detail), 1991-92, fibreglass and pigment, 91.5 diam x 76.2 cm*

ACADEMY EDITIONS · LONDON

Acknowledgements

'It's like listening to music . . . and feeling somehow fulfilled – that what you experienced was somehow extraordinary. It sustained you for a while . . . It is a sense of wonder and well-being that is projected by the art, whether music or painting or poetry.' **Robert Ryman**

'I don't feel that I'm being unfaithful to music when I'm drawing . . . I think everyone would benefit from drawing.' **John Cage**

'[Rauschenberg] had gone off to thrift shops and gotten all kinds of marvellous things. He dragged out a fur coat at one point and said, "Could you use this?" and I said "Of course," not having the slightest idea what I was going to do with it, but I obviously was going to use it – it looked alive . . . What we have done in our work is to bring together three separate elements in time and space, the music, the dance and the decor . . . The idea of a single focus to which all adhere is no longer relevant. With the paintings of Jackson Pollock the eye can go any place on the canvas. No one point is more important than another.' **Merce Cunningham**

'There was a shoot where I was trying to get David Parsons into the air. But he had stopped listening to me and had dropped to the floor and started to crawl across the floor, and I shot him doing this. To me, it's one of the strongest dance photographs I've taken. And I never would have dreamed of shooting a dancer crawling across a floor.' **Annie Leibovitz**

With thanks to the artists, photographers, writers, choreographers, galleries and institutions whose generous contributions have made this publication possible. **Front Cover**: Courtesy Laurie Lewis. **Inside Front Cover**: Courtesy Annie Leibovitz. **Inside Back Cover**: Courtesy Lois Greenfield; **Half-Title Page:** Courtesy Anthony d'Offay Gallery, London. **Frontis**: Courtesy Lisson Gallery, London. **Title Page**: Courtesy Val Wilmer. **Contents**: Courtesy Willard & Barbara Morgan Archives, Morgan Press, Dobbs Ferry, New York 10522. **Parade: A Scandalous Affair** pp6-15: With thanks to the author, Charles Spencer, for researching and providing much of the visual material for this piece. Thanks also to the Musée Picasso, Paris and the Theatre Museum, London. Images on pp6 & 12(below) courtesy the Board of Trustees of the Victoria & Albert Museum, London; pp9(above), 12(above) & 14(above) Musée Picasso, © RMN – SPADEM, Paris. **Merce Cunningham** pp16-23: With grateful thanks to David Vaughan, Archivist at the Cunningham Dance Foundation in New York, for writing the introduction to this piece, and for his kind assistance; and to Merce Cunningham and Marion Boyars for their permission to publish passages from *The Dancer and the Dance* (Marion Boyars Publishers, London & New York, revised and updated 1991). Barbara Morgan's photograph of Cunningham courtesy Willard & Barbara Morgan Archives, Morgan Press, New York. With thanks to Lloyd Morgan for his kind assistance and to James Klosty and Jack Mitchell for permission to publish their photographs. Images on p18 courtesy Margarete Roeder Gallery, New York; pp21 & 22 courtesy Cunningham Dance Foundation, New York. **John Cage: *Rolywholyover A Circus*** pp24-33: With thanks to Julie Lazar, Curator at MOCA, Los Angeles, for giving her time to the interview, and for sending visual material; image on p24 courtesy James Klosty; pp26-27 and p31 courtesy Estate of John Cage and Margarete Roeder Gallery, New York; p28 Anthony d'Offay Gallery, London; p30 & 33 MOCA, Los Angeles. Thanks also to Sadie Coles, of the Anthony d'Offay Gallery, for her assistance in the early stages of researching this piece. **John Cage: Paying Attention** pp34-39: With thanks to the author, Anne d'Harnoncourt, Director of the Philadelphia Museum of Art, for her permission to publish this text, first published in the *Rolywholyover A Circus* box publication, 1993; all images courtesy MOCA. **The Blow of the Sublime** pp40-41: With thanks to the author, Susan Sontag, for her permission to publish this abridged version of her 1987 text. **Annie Leibovitz: A Perfect Obsession** pp42-51: With thanks to Annie Leibovitz for giving her time to the interview, and to Lisa Mansourian for her assistance; all images courtesy Annie Leibovitz. **Anish Kapoor: Theatre of Lightness, Space and Intimacy** pp52-59: With thanks to Anish Kapoor for giving his time to the interview, and to the Lisson Gallery, London, in particular Emma Sandbach, for arranging the interview and for supplying all the visual material. **Laurie Booth: The Making of River Run** pp60-61: With thanks to Laurie Booth for agreeing to talk about his work and to Jane Quinn for her kind assistance. **Robert Ryman: A Sequence of Variations** pp62-67: Thanks to Robert Ryman and The Pace Gallery, New York, for permission to publish statements by the artist in this article; image on p62 courtesy the Lisson Gallery; p64 The Museum of Modern Art, New York; pp65&66 The Pace Gallery, New York. Thanks also to Catherine Kinley of the Tate Gallery for her assistance. **Val Wilmer: Shooting the Blues** pp68-75: Thanks to The Special Photographers Company, London, and to Val Wilmer for giving her time to the interview. **Jan Vercruysse: Sounds of Silence** pp76-79: All images kindly supplied by the Lisson Gallery, London. **Moments in Time: A Century of Dance Photography** pp80-87: Images on pp80 & 82-83 courtesy Laurie Lewis; pp84-85 courtesy Chris Nash and the Akehurst Gallery, London; p87 Nijinsky photograph courtesy the Board of Trustees of the Victoria & Albert Museum, London; Barbara Morgan's photograph of Martha Graham and Morgan's statement (from her *Oral History*, UCLA, 1972) on *Letter to the World* courtesy Willard & Barbara Morgan Archives, Morgan Press, New York. **The Phenomenology of Dance** pp88-89: Image courtesy the Board of Trustees of the Victoria & Albert Museum. **Liberating the Dancer from the Dance** pp90-96: All images kindly supplied by Lois Greenfield.

COVER: Laurie Lewis, Viviana Durante rehearsing her role in La Ronde, *1993, detail of photograph on pages 62-63*
INSIDE FRONT COVER: Annie Leibovitz, Bill T Jones, *1993, see pages 42-43*

HOUSE EDITOR: Nicola Hodges SENIOR DESIGNER: Andrea Bettella
DESIGN CO-ORDINATOR: Mario Bettella DESIGN TEAM: Jacqueline Grosvenor, Jason Rigby

First published in Great Britain in 1993 by *Art & Design* an imprint of the
ACADEMY GROUP LTD, 42 LEINSTER GARDENS, LONDON W2 3AN
MEMBER OF THE VCH PUBLISHING GROUP

ISBN: 1 85490 216 4

Art & Design Profile 33 is published as part of *Art & Design* Vol 8 11/12 1993
Art & Design Magazine is published six times a year and is available by subscription

Printed and bound in Italy

Contents

Barbara Morgan, Merce Cunningham, Root of an Unfocus, *1944*

ART & DESIGN PROFILE No 33

PARALLEL STRUCTURES

Guest-Edited by Clare Farrow

Serge Diaghilev in Paris, signed and dated 1928

PARADE

A SCANDALOUS AFFAIR
by Charles Spencer

*P*assing through the Italian town of Rovereto recently, I stopped to revisit the Depero Museum. The career of this Futurist artist included paintings, theatre designs, posters, commercial advertisements, packagings, fabrics and furniture. The top floor is devoted to a huge model of the setting which he devised in 1916 for Stravinsky's ballet *Le Chant du Rossignol*. A grotesque plastic garden, it recalls the devouring vegetation of Hollywood science-fiction. The displayed costume designs combine Chinese motifs with angular mechanism. Alongside are the marionettes which Depero created two years later for his *Plastic Ballets*, clearly suggesting the influence of Gordon Craig, the daring theatrical innovator who from Florence, as early as 1913, was advocating a marionette theatre.

Stravinsky's opera *Le Rossignol* was presented by Diaghilev in 1914 with designs by Alexandre Benois. For the ballet version choreographed by Massine he approached Fortunato Depero, but the eventual production was delayed until 1920, when it was designed by Matisse.

The Italian artist was to suffer a second rejection by Diaghilev. For the 1917 *Contes Russes*, designed by Larionov, Depero was instructed to create a model horse. Massine describes a visit to the artist's studio where he was presented with 'a bulbous outsized elephant'. Diaghilev, 'in a sudden outburst of rage, smashed the papier-mâché animal with his walking stick.'

The impresario was more successful with the older Futurist painter Giacomo Balla who devised the famous mechanised light-show for a performance of Stravinsky's *Fireworks* at the Constanzi Theatre, Rome, in 1917. Three years earlier Balla had produced a Futurist ballet, *The Typewriter*, in which performers moved with mechanical gestures to the sound of a writing machine. Here again the prophet is Gordon Craig who as early as 1909 advocated 'an abstract synthesis of movement, sound and light,' taking 'its expression chiefly from changes in lighting as it strikes a number of shapes.'

In studying the genesis of *Parade*, it is necessary to note the daring experiments which preceded it. In the world of art and ideas there are no virgin births. Appia and Craig sought the domination of design and even the elimination of live performers. The revolutionary achievements of the Futurists in confrontational performance, music and design were to be immensely influential. Diaghilev was aware of these developments. In 1911 he experienced Appia's innovations in decor and lighting at the Dalcroze School in Switzerland, and at one stage he actually announced Craig's collaboration on a ballet, *Cupid and Psyche*, which never materialised. It is fascinating to imagine which of these two egocentrics would have survived such a close working encounter.

Both in Paris and Italy, Diaghilev was acquainted with the Futurists. A drawing by Cangiullo depicts him with Stravinsky, attending a performance at Marinetti's house in Milan. In March 1915 Diaghilev wrote to Stravinsky about the 'concrete music' of the Futurists.

Most of the elements which made up *Parade* can be found in Futurist manifestos on theatre and music, from 1911 onwards, the elements of music-hall, circus, silent cinema and machine. Cocteau wanted the ballet to 'distil the involuntary emotion given off by circuses, music-halls, carousels, public balls, factories, seaports, the movies . . .' and he instructed Satie to incorporate into the music 'the noises of dynamos, sirens, express trains, aeroplanes, typewriters,' echoing Russolo's 1913 manifesto *The Art of Noises*. Furthermore, in imitation of Marinetti, Cocteau wished to participate as narrator.

One must also acknowledge the immense influence of Futurism in Russia. Marinetti paid two visits to the country, at the invitation of Larionov, and inspired a national movement led by Mayakovsky and David Burliuk. This culminated in the Futurist Festival in Luna Park, St Petersburg, in 1913, when Mayakovsky presented and acted in *A Tragedy*; and the first Futurist opera, *Victory over the Sun*, which was designed by Malevich. The performers, dehumanised by masks and lighting, resembled mechanistic elements, and the Cubo-Futurist sets eventually led to geometric abstraction.

With his deep love for Russia and his lasting fascination for theatrical experiments, Diaghilev kept abreast of these events and later introduced Russian Constructivism into ballet via the work of Tchelitchew, Gabo and Yacoulov.

There was an intimation of things to come in Nijinsky's ballet *Jeux*, of 1913, said to be based on a game of tennis in a Bloomsbury square. A contemporary critic referred to Nijinsky pushing himself and his two female partners into 'Cubist contortions, twisting Karsavina's precious limbs in the name of Matisse, Metzinger and Picasso.'

ABOVE: Henri Matisse with Léonide Massine in Monte Carlo, 1920, preparing Stravinsky's ballet Le Chant du Rossignol

 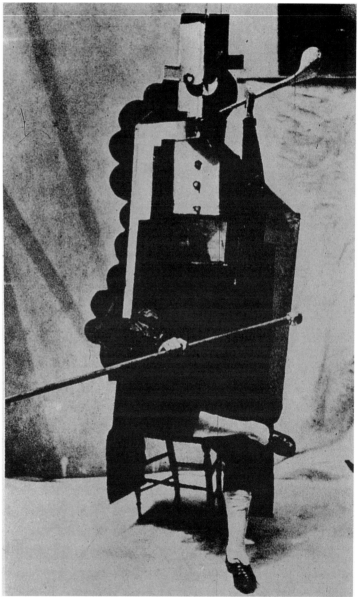

LEFT: The American Manager, Parade, *1917; RIGHT: The French Manager,* Parade, *1917*

The 'true begetter' of *Parade* was Jean Cocteau. At the age of 20 he witnessed the first performance of the Ballets Russes in 1909 and eventually met Diaghilev through their mutual friend, Misia Sert. In 1910 he published a volume of poems dedicated to Nijinsky (probably to Diaghilev's alarm). He charmed Léon Bakst, who drew his portrait and promoted his poster designs for *Le Spectre de la Rose*, 1911. (Characteristically, Cocteau later reciprocated by calling Bakst 'a huge society Parakeet . . . a monster of Jewish duplicity.') Then in 1912 Diaghilev accepted Cocteau's libretto for *Le Dieu Bleu*.

There were other reasons why Cocteau sought the Diaghilev milieu. Stravinsky commented, 'It is almost impossible to describe the perversity of Diaghilev's entourage . . . a kind of homosexual Swiss Guard . . .' 'For me they were a family,' Cocteau confessed, the first substitute he had found for his own bourgeois background. Then came the famous incident of 'Etonnez-moi!' Cocteau repeatedly told the story, of an evening in 1912, when he was crossing the Place de la Concorde with Diaghilev and Nijinsky, feeling some coldness towards himself. When he questioned Diaghilev the reply was, 'Astound me! I'll wait for you to astound me.' 'Finally,' Cocteau later claimed, 'in 1917, the opening night of *Parade,* I did astound him.' It had taken him five years to do so.

Cocteau said that the idea for the ballet came to him in 1916 while listening to Satie playing his *Morceaux en forme de poire* (Three Pieces in the Form of a Pear). Shortly afterwards he defined the word *parade* as 'a burlesque scene played outside a sideshow booth to entice spectators.' He enlarged the outline in a series of notes to Satie, referring to a Chinese magician, the American Girl and an acrobat, advising the composer to create a score in which sounds could be combined with words.

In fact the idea had been developed by Cocteau two years previously for a projected ballet called *David*, which he hoped would 'astound' Diaghilev. At that time he sketched the action: 'On stage, in front of a booth at the fair, an acrobat would be doing a come-on for *David*, a spectacle intended to be given inside the booth. A clown, who is later transformed into a box (theatrical pastiche of a phonograph played at fairs – modern form of the ancient mask) was to celebrate David's exploits through a loudspeaker and urge the public to enter the booth and see the show.' Clearly this is the origin of *Parade*. Cocteau tried to persuade Stravinsky to write the score. He intended to design the ballet, and to write and recite the verbal accompaniment. Both the composer and Diaghilev turned him down.

In a subsequent letter to Misia Sert, he affirmed, '*David's* failure surely served to make possible the birth of the new work.' He also recalled the fairground ballet *Petrushka* in the hope of giving his new work a similar universal appeal.

By 1916 he had met Picasso and was posing for a portrait in uniform – said to have been designed by

Poiret. He accompanied the painter on a visit to Apollinaire who was in hospital, suffering from a head wound. Françoise Gilot tells us, 'Whilst he [Picasso] was alone one day in his atelier, Jean Cocteau, dressed as Harlequin, had come to tell him he felt it was time Pablo came down out of his ivory tower and took Cubism out into the street, or at least into the theatre . . .' Cocteau realised that with Satie and Picasso on his side, it might well be possible to astound Diaghilev.

Picasso had not previously worked in the theatre and had even less interest in ballet. The decision to involve himself in, and eventually to dominate Cocteau's conception, resulted from complex personal and aesthetic needs. He had long been attracted to performers and especially to circus people, as he expressed in numerous studies and such masterpieces as *The Family of Acrobats with Ape* and *Family of Saltimbanques*, both painted in 1905. The attraction continued. In 1910 his mistress Fernande Olivier wrote to Gertrude Stein, '. . . we have become great friends with some clowns, acrobats, circus riders and dancers.' And Max Jacob, staying with Picasso at Céret in 1913, recorded, 'A travelling circus has arrived . . . we are charmed with this gay little crowd.'

In 1916 Picasso began to make studies of circus performers and also completed elegant portraits of Max Jacob and Apollinaire in the 'Ingres' style. These suggest a perhaps unspoken, even unpremeditated, desire for change.

The period 1915-16 was very difficult for Picasso personally. Braque and other close friends were at the front, and his mistress Eva (Marcelle Humbert) died after a long illness. The 34-year-old artist was miserable and lonely, a state which he masochistically exasperated by moving to the suburb of Montrouge. On lonely night-time walks home from Montparnasse he was often accompanied by his old friend Satie who lived further out, in Arcueil. The eccentric composer had at one time played the piano at *Le Chat Noir* in Montparnasse, and had been the lover of Suzanne Valadon, the future mother of Maurice Utrillo.

In 1915 Cocteau was introduced to Picasso by Edgar Varèse and immediately fell under the Spaniard's spell – for life! In turn Picasso was charmed by the wit and elegance of this young Frenchman, eight years his junior. In time Cocteau would occupy the role of jester in Picasso's court.

As Françoise Gilot again informs us, Cocteau regularly tried to cajole Picasso into designing his new ballet. 'To the astonishment of all and with the insistent disapproval of serious-minded Cubists,' writes Roland Penrose, 'Picasso accepted.' Cocteau recalled, 'In Montparnasse in 1916, it was in the middle of the street between the Rotonde and the Dôme that I asked Picasso to do *Parade* . . . The artists around him couldn't believe that he would go along with me . . . to paint a stage set for a Russian

ABOVE: Pablo Picasso, 1904; BELOW: Léonide Massine in Legend of Joseph, *1914*

Programme des Ballets Russes

Costume de Chinois du ballet "PARADE"
Aquarelle de Picasso

Pablo Picasso, the Chinese Conjurer, Parade, 1917, watercolour

ballet was a crime. Picasso scandalised the Café de la Rotonde in accepting my invitation.' Cocteau was to learn to regret it.

It is less clear at what stage Diaghilev accepted the work. He had admired Satie's piano compositions in 1914 at the house of Misia Sert. But it was not until May 1916 that the composer met Diaghilev. The two giants impressed one another. Diaghilev's situation was drastically affected by the war, not only the lack of funds, patrons, venues and audiences, which resulted in periods in Spain and Italy, but also the more emotional break with his Russian roots and inspiration, later deepened by the Revolution. According to Prince Peter Lieven, historian of the Ballets Russes, 'After the war . . . the united group, with whose members Diaghilev had reached maturity, whose leader he was, no longer existed. To remain the protagonist of all that was progressive in art he had to go and seek for advancement, had to attract to his service collaborators who already had the hallmark of *le dernier cri*.' Diaghilev was ruthless in abandoning old colleagues when they no longer served his purposes.

Involving major painters in the theatre was by no means Diaghilev's invention. He modelled himself on Sava Marmontov, the Russian railway tycoon who opened Moscow's first private opera company in the 1880s and persuaded his painter friends, including the great artist Vrubel, to design productions. Marmontov financed Diaghilev's art magazine *Mir Isskustva* in 1898 and inspired Bakst and Benois, among others, to work in the theatre. There were similar movements in other parts of Europe, notably Max Reinhardt's collaboration with leading Viennese and German painters. In 1906-7 he invited Edvard Munch to design plays by Ibsen.

Following the break from Russia, Diaghilev began to turn to European collaborators; to the Spanish painter Sert, to composers such as Claude Debussy and Richard Strauss, even to Bonnard who designed the poster for *Legend of Joseph* in 1914. The opportunity of working with Picasso, therefore, must have seemed a godsend. Diaghilev sought change, not only because of his infamous boredom and need for stimulation, and the satisfaction of bringing together artists of great talent, whom he could finally dominate, but above all to feed the constant search for publicity and new audiences which were essential if the company was to survive.

With Satie and Picasso on his side, Cocteau fielded a strong team. They met with Diaghilev on 7 October 1916, together with the choreographer Massine. 'I have the impression that Serge likes our work,' Cocteau reported, 'and understands perfectly the seemingly simple motivation I provided for the union between musician and painter.' Diaghilev was to favour a union between painter and choreographer. On 11 January 1917 Picasso wrote to Diaghilev:

Confirming our verbal agreement, I accept to undertake the production (sets, curtains, cos-

tumes and properties) for the ballet *Parade* by Jean Cocteau and Erik Satie. I will make all the necessary designs and models and I will personally supervise all the work of carrying them out. All the designs will be ready by 15 March 1917. For this work you are to pay me the sum of five thousand francs, and if I have to go to Rome, a thousand francs extra. The drawings and model remain my property. Half the sum named must be paid on delivery of the designs and models, and the other half on the day of the first performance.

Cocteau wrote similar letters on behalf of Satie and himself. A month later, Diaghilev invited the trio to Rome for preparations and rehearsals. Satie refused to leave Paris, but Picasso and Cocteau went.

Cocteau had enlarged the *David* concept with a series of turns outside a sideshow, designed to entice spectators inside. The protagonists of *Parade* are a Chinese magician who juggles with eggs out of his pigtail; the Little American Girl, based on Mary Pickford, who enacts scenes from silent movies, including an imitation of Charlie Chaplin; and a male Acrobat, to whom a female was added to facilitate Massine's melancholic *pas-de-deux*. The final dénouement is their failure to attract an audience.

Cocteau had two basic requirements: that Satie should compose music which included Futurist sounds, and that he, Cocteau, would intone commentaries through a megaphone: 'Come and see the truth about America, the earthquakes, the short-circuits, the Hudson detectives, Ragtime, factories, derailed trains, sinking steamers. A moment's hesitation and you're lost.'

Satie, and more importantly Picasso, had other ideas. On 4 September 1916 Cocteau begged his friend Valentine Gross, 'Make Satie understand that I do count for something in *Parade* and that he and Picasso are not the only ones involved. It hurts me when he dances round Picasso screaming, 'It's you I'm following. You are the master . . .' Ten days later Satie reported to Valentine, '*Parade* is changing for the better, behind Cocteau's back. Picasso has ideas that I like better than our Jean's and I am all for Picasso. And Jean doesn't know it. Picasso tells me to go ahead, following Jean's text, and he, Picasso, will work on another text, his own . . .'

Picasso's main innovation, apart from the actual designing, was the introduction of three new characters, the Managers, who acted as barkers in presenting the acts to the passing public. These were non-dancing parts since their principal purpose was to wear and present Picasso's monstrous ten-feet Cubist constructions, virtually walking decors. Massine was required to invent stomping and foot-stamping, which was about all the Managers were capable of doing. The French Manager carried a massive structure on which was represented a man with curving moustaches,

Pablo Picasso, the Acrobat, Parade, *1917, watercolour and pencil*

ABOVE: Pablo Picasso, overture curtain for Parade, *1917, tempera on canvas, 10 x 17 m; BELOW: Léonide Massine as the Chinese Conjurer in* Parade, *1917*

wearing evening dress and an opera hat, and carrying a long white pipe and a walking stick. The American Manager was a curious mixture of the Wild West and President Lincoln, with cowboy boots, a tall stove-pipe hat, a vision of skyscrapers, a megaphone and a panel bearing the word PARADE. The third Manager was less defined, a dummy or marionette of a negro in evening dress, mounted on a grotesque horse, created on the backs of two performers. Its faulty construction resulted in a sagging back so that the dummy regularly fell off in rehearsal. It was finally dumped.

Other important deviations included the music and the vocal commentary. Satie refused to incorporate the Futurist sounds, although he did use a typewriter, and was totally against the use of words. His score was typically satirical and mysterious, with jaunty jazz rhythms, described by Ansermet as 'learned popular music'. Cocteau had to wait for the Ballets Suédois and *Les Mariés de la Tour Eiffel* in 1921 before he was allowed to recite through a backstage horn. (The innovation was later adopted by Frederick Ashton for Edith Sitwell's *Façade*, 1931, and *Wedding Bouquet*, 1937, with recitations of Gertrude Stein's verse.)

There was a more fundamental difference between Cocteau and Picasso. In the original conception Cocteau referred to an 'occult element' and suggested dramatic undertones in 'the Chinaman capable of torture, the Little Girl drowned on *The Titanic*, Acrobats communing with stars.' Picasso cut through such pretensions to create something brash, earthy, witty and finally meaningless. Cocteau objected, 'There is nothing intentionally humorous in my outline,' but in the end he lost control, and the battle.

Douglas Cooper, the most authoritative writer on Picasso's theatrical work, suggests that the artist arrived in Rome with positive ideas for the decor and the drop curtain, as well as for the costumes. He set up a studio on the Via Margutta, while rehearsals took place in the Cantina Taglioni on the Piazza Venezia. They all worked hard, 'snatching our meals between working and walking,' according to Cocteau, 'and falling asleep exhausted.' Nevertheless there was time for sight-seeing and visits to museums, including a trip to Naples and Pompeii. The effect on Picasso of Roman sculpture and Michelangelo can be seen in his emergent neoclassical period.

There is fascinating speculation about the composition of Picasso's famous front curtain. It is obvious that it looks back to his earlier circus compositions. There is the same sympathetic, sweet, romantic manner, now presented in the flat, almost naive style of a theatrical poster.

An off-stage scene is indicated in sections of the scenery and curtains. The performers are rehearsing or resting. Around a table a torrero strums his guitar, together with a blackamoor, harlequins, a sailor and two women. Before them a dog is curled up asleep. On the other side a winged dancer strides the back of a winged horse, which is gently nudging its foal, overlooked by a monkey at the top of a ladder. It is all delightfully relaxed, free of tension or disturbance. Perhaps it is entirely appropriate before a *parade*.

For years I have heard a suggestion that Picasso borrowed the scene or the composition from a postcard purchased in Naples. Dr Marianne Martin, of New York University, asserts that the curtain is based on a fresco in the Naples Aquarium, *Friends in a Pergola*, painted by the German artist Hans von Marees in 1873. Nesta Macdonald, on the other hand, traces its origins to Mancinelli's painted curtain in the San Carlo Opera House. Could it be that Picasso obtained a postcard of one of these compositions? None of his biographers refers to this.

Nesta Macdonald goes even further, playfully suggesting that this unpretentious assembly is really a Picassian joke. The blackamoor, she argues, is Stravinsky – à la *Petrushka*; the harlequin is Matisse; the bare-back rider is Lopokova; the sailor is Diaghilev (because he feared the sea, or is there a corny 'hello sailor' joke there?); Picasso is the torrero – of course; and alongside him one of the women is the dancer Olga Kokhlova, later to become the artist's wife.

As one might expect, there are equally divergent reports of the première of *Parade* at the Théâtre du Châtelet in Paris on 18 May, 1917, at 3.45pm, a benefit for war-time charities. The motley audience included some of Diaghilev's patrons – the Princess de Polignac, Countess Greffulhe, Etiénne de Beaumont, and his friend Misia Sert. He had also invited a group of Russian soldiers on leave from the Western Front. Complimentary tickets were issued to Juan Gris and Severini, to Apollinaire and the composers Poulenc and Auric. The bulk of the audience were devotees of ballet and admirers of the Ballets Russes.

The charming front curtain was greeted with admiration and applause. Satie's music may have been confusing, but there were constant echoes of music-hall songs and popular dances. To begin with, painters and musicians in the audience were enthusiastic. 'Vive Picasso!' they shouted, 'Vive Satie!' But the mood changed dramatically when the curtain rose to reveal the asymmetrical decor, with its Cubist proscenium framed by skyscrapers; and although the performers' costumes were colourfully acceptable, the mountainous structures for the Managers and their mechanistic stamping outraged sections of the audience. Cries of 'Salles Boches' rang through the theatre, a disturbing reminder that some 150 miles away wartime slaughter continued.

The ballet lasted 20 minutes, the uproar that followed 15. Cocteau, determined to exaggerate the

FROM ABOVE: Jean Cocteau in Les Mariés de la Tour Eiffel, *1921; Pablo Picasso, Erik Satie,1920; Erik Satie, part of the score for* Parade, *1917*

débâcle, exclaimed, 'I have heard the cries of the bayonet charge in Flanders, but it was nothing to what happened that night at the Châtelet. He claimed that he and Picasso were rescued from an angry mob by Apollinaire in army uniform, with head bandaged.

There were calmer reports. According to Paul Morand, 'A full house yesterday at the Châtelet for *Parade*. Canvas scenery in the circus style by Picasso; pretty music by Satie. The Managers . . . were surprising. The Little American Girl and the acrobatic dancers had charming costumes. Massine too as the Chinese juggler. Much applause and a few whistles.'

The critics ranged from dismissive to insulting. When one viciously attacked Satie's music, the composer sent him a postcard: 'Monsieur et cher ami, you're no more than an arse, an arse without music.' Cocteau was compensated by a note from Marcel Proust: 'I cannot tell you how delighted I am at the considerable stir made by your ballet.'

Cocteau, however, remained furious at what he considered to have been the theft of his ideas, the weak response of Satie to Picasso's domination, and Diaghilev's encouragement of the Picasso/Massine partnership at his expense. He wrote to a friend, 'I could give you a picture of myself spitting in Diaghilev's face in Rome . . .'

His sense of injury was only increased by Apollinaire's programme note, based on a previously printed newspaper article. The advocate of Cubism was full of praise for his friend Picasso, for Satie and Massine, but he barely mentioned Cocteau. This essay is now largely remembered for Apollinaire's substitution of the term *ballet réaliste* for *sur-réaliste*, thereby predicting a new movement.

Cocteau was never reconciled to the elimination of what he considered to be vital elements, especially his vocal commentary. He hated the Managers and 'their towering carcasses'. '*Parade* was so far from what I would have wished that I never went to see it out front.' When the ballet was revived in 1920 he attempted to reverse previous decisions. 'Cocteau is repeating his tiresome antics of 1917,' wrote Satie. 'He is being such a nuisance to Picasso and me that I feel quite knocked out. It's a mania with him. *Parade* is his alone. That's all right with me. But why didn't he do the sets and the costumes and write the music for this poor ballet.'

Removed from the creative conflicts and the first-night uproar, the ballet was clearly lightweight. Juan Gris considered it unpretentious, 'a sort of musical joke,' and Gide, typically bitchy, commented, 'Hard to say what is more striking, the pretentiousness or the poverty.' Performed by the Ballets Russes until 1926, the ballet was restaged by Massine in 1962, since when there have been occasional performances in America and Europe.

Parade initiated a new experimental era for the Ballets Russes, with a procession of avant-garde painter-designers – Matisse, Braque, Juan Gris, Derain, Marie Laurencin, Rouault, De Chirico, Max Ernst, and others. They in turn inspired leading artists to contribute to their own national theatres. Some felt that this revolution was not entirely beneficial, leading to the subjugation of dance to decoration. It cannot be mere coincidence that unlike the earlier Russian productions, very few of Diaghilev's post-war ballets have found permanent places in the repertoire.

Picasso, the dominant creator of *Parade*, may also be judged to have been its chief beneficiary. It brought him into the theatre; he continued to contribute to the Ballets Russes until 1924 and worked for the theatre well into the 50s. It brought him his first wife, Olga Kokhlova, and his first son, Paulo. At a period of depression, *Parade* proved to be a therapeutic diversion. Misia Sert considered that '*Parade* was Picasso's first contact with the general public.' The publicity resulted in new exhibitions and collectors. Roland Penrose wrote, 'Picasso had influenced the ballet, but the ballet was also to have its influence on him. Not only did it give him the chance to paint on a larger scale than had been possible hitherto, and to see his costumes and constructions realised, and moving in space and light, but it also brought him into close relationship with the human form.'

Above all, his first experience of Italy, the weeks in Rome, and the visits to Naples and Pompeii, provided the stimulus for the stylistic change he clearly desired, the period of neo-classicism. Curiously enough, Diaghilev and ballet were also the beneficiaries. Preparing *Le Train Bleu* in 1924, Diaghilev was dissatisfied with the setting by sculptor Henri Laurens. How could he give it that extra excitement? He remembered a painting in Picasso's studio, *The Race*, depicting two neo-classical giantesses running on a beach. He obtained the artist's permission to blow up the scene as an appropriate front curtain for a ballet concerned with sea-side frolics.

Bibliography

Futurism: Caroline Tisdall and Angelo Bozzola
Picasso Theatre: Douglas Cooper
Life with Picasso: François Gilot and Carlton Lake
Picasso: Roland Penrose
Cocteau: Francis Steegmuller
The Birth of the Ballets Russes: Prince Peter Lieven
The Diaghilev Ballet: SL Grigoriev
Diaghilev: Arnold Haskell
Diaghilev: Richard Buckle

The World of Serge Diaghilev: Charles Spencer
Léon Bakst: Charles Spencer
Diaghilev Observed: Nesta Macdonald
One or Three Muses: Misia Sert
Art in Modern Ballet: George Amberg
Art and the Stage: Edited by Henning Rischbeiter
Revolutions in Stage Design in the XXth Century: Denis Bablet
Design for the Ballet: Mary Clarke and Clement Crisp

OPPOSITE FROM ABOVE: Pablo Picasso with assistants during the making of the front curtain for Parade, *1917;* Parade *set, 1917; Picasso with Olga Kokhlova in London, 1919*

MERCE CUNNINGHAM

THOUGHTS ON DANCE, MUSIC & THE VISUAL ARTS
Introduction by David Vaughan

The mind will say, 'Oh, I cannot do that', but if you try it, a lot of the time you can do it, and even if you can't, it shows you something you didn't know before. Merce Cunningham

Merce Cunningham was born in Centralia, a small town in the state of Washington, in the Northwest United States, in 1919. His first dance studies were with Mrs Maude Barrett, a local teacher of tap and ballroom dance. After high school and a year of college, Cunningham attended the Cornish School in Seattle (now called Cornish College) with the idea of becoming an actor, but dance classes with Bonnie Bird, a former member of the Martha Graham Company, convinced him that he should become a dancer.

It was at Cornish, in 1938, that Merce Cunningham met John Cage, whom Bonnie Bird had engaged as musician for the dance department. In the summer of 1939 Bird, Cunningham and other of her students attended a summer school at Mills College in Oakland, California, at which Martha Graham saw Cunningham dance and offered him a place in her company. Cunningham quit school and went to New York, where he became the second male member of Graham's company, in which he was to remain until 1945.

Even before he left Graham, Cunningham began to choreograph independently. In 1942 he and two other members of the Graham company, Jean Erdman and Nina Fonaroff, shared a concert at Bennington College in Vermont, where the company was in residence for the summer. John Cage by this time had also moved east, and wrote a score for *Credo in Us*, which Cunningham and Erdman choreographed and danced together. This work marks the beginning of Cunningham's lifelong collaboration with Cage.

Two years later the two men gave a concert together in New York City, in which Cunningham danced six solos, all with music by Cage. In those solos they moved closer toward the principle of independence of dance and music; choreography and music were composed according to an agreed rhythmic structure, coming together at certain key points but otherwise pursuing an independent course.

Cunningham's dissatisfaction with Graham's way of working was growing, and in 1945 he left her company. He and Cage continued to give yearly concerts in New York, and also began to tour across the United States. An important commission came to them in 1947 from Lincoln Kirstein: for Ballet Society, the forerunner of New York City Ballet, they created *The Seasons*, with designs by Isamu Noguchi, who had designed many works for Martha Graham. (Cunningham and Cage originally wanted the Northwestern artist Morris Graves to design the piece.)

In 1948 Cunningham and Cage visited Black Mountain College, the progressive liberal arts school in North Carolina, for the first time. They were to return two or three times in the next few years: in 1952 Cage put on the famous untitled, unstructured theatre piece, generally considered to be the prototype of the artists' 'happenings' of the 1960s; in 1953 Cunningham took with him to the school a number of dancers he had been working with in New York, including Carolyn Brown, Viola Farber, Remy Charlip and Paul Taylor. They rehearsed a repertory of dances that they performed at the end of the summer, and Cunningham decided to keep them together as a company.

Cunningham and Cage were friendly with the painters of the New York School – Cunningham's decentralisation of the stage space had something in common with the kind of spatial composition found in the paintings of Jackson Pollock, for example, where no area of the canvas is more important than any other. But they felt a more immediate rapport with younger painters like Robert Rauschenberg and Jasper Johns. Rauschenberg had been at Black Mountain, and the all-white paintings he made there encouraged Cage to write his important silent piece, *4'33"*. Rauschenberg made his first set for Cunningham in 1954 (*Minutiae*). For the next ten years he was the company's resident designer and, eventually, stage manager.

In the early 1950s John Cage had begun to investigate the use of chance processes in musical composition, and Cunningham sought ways to apply them to choreography. By such methods as tossing coins, he found the sequence of movement phrases in a dance, where in the space they would occur, how many dancers would perform them, and how many times.

By this time the independence of dance and music had become absolute; though Cunningham still worked with time structures, length of duration was the only thing the two had in common. The principles of musical or narrative form usually followed in dance composition were abandoned;

OPPOSITE: Leap, *1942, photo Barbara Morgan*

structure, rather than being preconceived, was organic. Cage and David Tudor, the company musician, and the composers who worked with them introduced a form of live electronic music, often using equipment that they themselves had devised.

In the first decade of the company's existence performances were few and far between. But in 1964 the company undertook a six-month world tour. Extended engagements in Paris and (especially) London received serious critical notice of a kind that had not been frequent in the United States. On their return home, Cunningham and his collaborators found a renewed interest in their work; domestic as well as foreign touring increased, and New York seasons eventually became an annual event.

Rauschenberg left the company after the 1964 tour. Jasper Johns assumed the title of artistic advisor, in which capacity he was responsible for a series of celebrated collaborations with visual artists such as Frank Stella, Andy Warhol, Robert Morris, Bruce Nauman, and himself. Johns also realised the decor for *Walkaround Time* (1968), based on Marcel Duchamp's *The Large Glass*. In 1980 the British painter Mark Lancaster succeeded Johns; he was already the company's *de facto* resident designer. Recent works have been designed by William Anastasi and Dove Bradshaw (the current artistic advisors), Lancaster, Carl Kielblock, and Marsha Skinner, among others.

Although Cunningham's physical capacities have declined, he still continues to 'appear' as he puts it, in almost every performance of the dance company, and there has been no diminution of his creative powers. Recently, he has choreographed as many as four new works each year. His interest in new technologies, already evinced in numerous works created specifically for video or film in collaboration with at first Charles Atlas, later Elliot Caplan, has been further demonstrated in his use of a computer programme, *Lifeforms*, as an adjunct to choreography. Even the death of John Cage in 1992, which clearly affected Cunningham both personally and professionally, caused no interruption in his intensive schedule of rehearsals and performances, touring and teaching.

Note

The following passages by Merce Cunningham have been selected from the choreographer's conversations with Jacqueline Lesschaeve, in *The Dancer and the Dance*, 1991, Marion Boyars Publishers, London and New York, and are reproduced here by kind permission of Merce Cunningham and Marion Boyars.

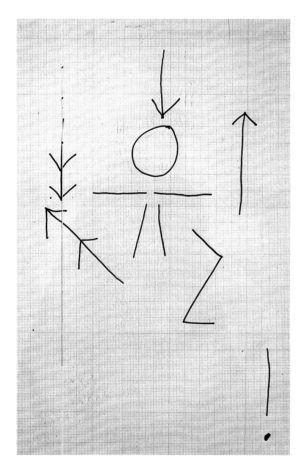

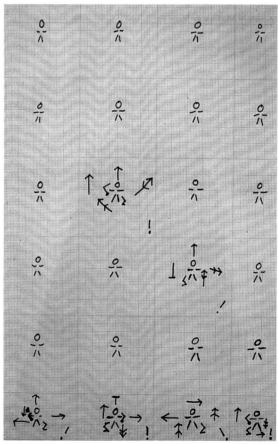

Unfinished Works, *1972, felt tip marker on graph paper, 2 pages, each 29.2 x 21.6 cm*

Space and Time

I used to be told that you see the centre of the space as the most important: that was the centre of interest. But in many modern paintings this was not the case and the sense of space was different. So I decided to open up the space to consider it equal, and any place, occupied or not, just as important as any other.

I began to work in that direction, for it opens up an enormous range of possibilities. As you're not referring one sequence to another you can constantly shift everything, the movement can be continuous, and numerous transformations can be imagined. You can still have people dancing the same phrase together, but they can also dance different phrases at the same time, different phrases divided in different ways, in two, three, five, eight or whatever. The space could be constantly fluid, instead of being a fixed space in which movements relate.

Suppose you now take the dimension of time. Our eight dancers can be doing different movements, they may even do them to the same rhythm which is all right, there's nothing wrong with any of it! – but there is also the possibility that they can be doing different movements in different rhythms, then that is where the real complexity comes in, adding this kind of material one on top of and with another.

Painters and Composers

It was during the war period that I saw (I didn't have much to do with them in the sense of friendship or anything of the kind) the paintings of Max Ernst and Marcel Duchamp and Piet Mondrian. But sometimes I would go to parties at Peggy Guggenheim's where they would be (John and Xenia Cage were staying with her and Max Ernst), and there were other artists who had come from abroad. That was a totally different world from the one that I knew through the Graham circle, and I expect that probably prompted me in some way to go and look at their work. Peggy Guggenheim had a gallery on 57th Street and I remember very often seeing shows there. She showed not only the surrealists but also younger artists.

I began to know the painting world and, through John Cage, the music world. By the time we gave the first programme together in 1944, the audience who came to see us was very small of course, but was composed of many of these painters. Very few dancers came, perhaps some of the Graham people came, I don't remember exactly. I do remember a number of painters coming and young composers, people interested in new possibilities.

I remember, for instance, hearing painters talk, not about dancing of course. I didn't know them well so I didn't say anything at these parties or gatherings, but they would talk about painting and this was interesting even though I knew nothing about it. I would listen and they would talk about their work, or somebody else's and the kind of talk was so different from anything I knew in the Graham world where talking was about technical things or what Martha might be doing or not doing.

Minutiae

Bob Rauschenberg had been at Black Mountain and John and I had met him there. There was a kind of compatibility about ideas and after we returned to New York we saw Bob a great deal and I realised we could probably work together. While I was making *Minutiae* I asked Bob if he'd do something visual for it. I didn't ask him for anything specific. I said that it might be something we could move through. He made an object which was very beautiful, hanging down from pipes, but I said, 'It's marvellous but we can't use it because we rarely play in theatres with flies.' He didn't get angry at all about it, he just said he'd make something else. I came back a few days later and he had made something else that was later exhibited. Wonderful object! Colours, comic strips all over it. You could pass through it or under it or round it. He made it out of stuff he'd picked up off the street. I loved it because it was impossible to know what it was.

Chance

I never thought and still don't, that dancing is intellectual. I think dancing is instinctual. No matter how complex something I make or do may be, if it doesn't come out as dancing it's of no use. I don't care about the diagrams – those are things that one does, that I need to do often with my pieces because of the complexity. But that's only the paper work – you have to get up and do it. When I give composition workshops, illustrating the ways to use chance, the students get so involved with the papers, the possibilities become so fascinating, I've always had to stop them, get them to give up the paper, get out there and work on it, otherwise it never materialises: it doesn't come alive.

The two questions they ask concerning the chance procedures are: 'If something comes up that you don't like, what do you do about it?' My answer to that always has been that I would accept and deal with what came up. And they ask, 'If something comes up that you can't do, then what do you do?' I explain that I would always try it, because the mind will say you can't do it, but more often than not you can, or you see another way, and that's what's amazing. In some cases it *is* impossible, but something else happens, some other possibility appears, and your mind opens.

Erik Satie

I can listen to Satie music now – for instance the *Three Pieces in the Form of A Pear*, which I have heard over and over for years, and it is still just as refreshing as the first time – whereas that doesn't happen to me with the music of other composers that I have listened to – I find very quickly that I begin to know the formal procedures, and it doesn't hold my interest as Satie's still does. The focus on Satie was brought by Cage.

Marcel Duchamp

Walkaround Time is my homage to Marcel Duchamp. When the idea came up about using *The Large Glass* for a set, I began to think about Marcel. I wasn't going to do something imitative, but it was going to be my reactions to him; I didn't think I could do anything else. There are many personal references to Marcel in that piece. There's one part of the dance where I'm at the back and I change my clothes running in place, because he was so concerned about motion and nudity. Then I knew the objects that would be *on* stage would be transparent although I had no idea how big they were going to be, because I never saw them until the day of the performance; but I knew that we could certainly be seen behind them, so I kept that in mind.

Marcel Duchamp had consented to the idea of having a set made from *The Large Glass* as long as Jasper was making it, and the only thing he asked was that it be assembled at one point in the dance, and I said certainly, so I did it at the end. The idea of the middle part, the entr'acte, comes from *Relâche*, where there is an entr'acte, with a movie in it. I wanted to make a long piece so I wanted to have an entr'acte, so to speak, to break it up in the middle.

The whole piece is forty-nine minutes, two parts and the entr'acte. The set consists of the seven objects of the *Glass*. They limited very much what one could do in the space.

The music is by David Behrman. There is a movie of it, made by Charles Atlas.

Stillness and Motion

My energy is nourished by motion. That is, thinking that even when one is still one is really in motion, so that one is constantly moving, one does not pose.

Antic Meet

Antic Meet is a series of absurd situations, one after the other, each one independent of the next. Bob Rauschenberg did the decor and the costumes. I remember talking with him, but I worked on it up in Connecticut, and he was in New York. At one point I told him that I wanted to have a chair on my back. He thought about it and said 'Okay.' (laughter) After a while he said, 'Well, if you have a chair, can I have a door?' and I said 'Sure, why not? Fine.' I also told him that in one part I wanted to wear a sweater which had four arms. That was all right. He said something about the girls wearing special dresses, and I said, 'It's fine, okay.' So he was making all these things, and I was up there, during the summer, trying to get the dance together. I came down to New York to see what he had done – he said I should. He had gone off to thrift shops and gotten all kinds of marvellous things. He dragged out a fur coat at one point and said, 'Could you use this?' and I said 'Of course,' not having the slightest idea what I was going to do with it, but I obviously was going to use it – it looked alive. Then he brought out a bouquet of artificial flowers, and said 'Could you use this?' and showed me how it

disappeared – it was from a magic shop – and I said, 'Absolutely, absolutely' – again not having the slightest idea. Then he put on one of these dresses that he had made from a parachute. (laughter) It looked like Givenchy – it was elegant and beautiful – it was made of nylon silk. I could see it would work wonderfully . . . And the door . . . I had said, 'Fine, if you want a door, that's fine, but how about getting one?' 'Oh, any theatre has a door,' was the answer. Bob came to Connecticut to work on all this a week or ten days before the performance – of course there wasn't a door. But that didn't stop Bob. He found one – built one with wheels – and this door, Carolyn would roll it on – she was behind it – you couldn't see her – and then I'd open it up, and there she was . . . (laughter) The music was John Cage's *Concert for Piano and Orchestra*. Very often on tour it would be done with the solo for piano alone, and David Tudor would play it.

OPPOSITE: Solo, *1973, photo Jack Mitchell; BELOW:* Antic Meet, *1958, photo Richard Rutledge*

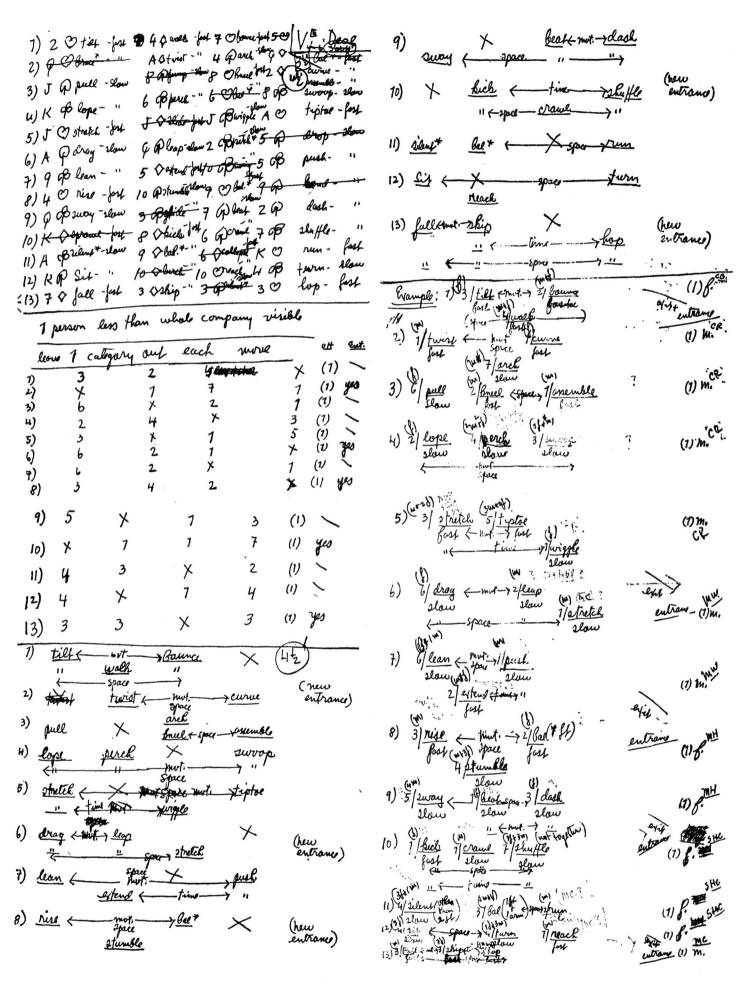

Canfield, *1969, list of movements*

A Game of Cards

Canfield, made in 1969, is a dance that in its entirety can last one hour and fifteen minutes. It is comprised of thirteen dances and of fourteen others that I call 'in-betweens'. The title is from the game of solitaire. While playing it one summer day on vacation in Cadaques I decided the procedure could be used for choreography. The various components of a deck of cards were allotted to aspects of dance. To each of the fifty-two cards I related a word that implied movement, for example, the Queen of Spades indicated leap; the Ten of Diamonds lurch; the Seven of Hearts bounce, continuing for all fifty-two. Then I used the idea of thirteen cards in a suit to indicate the number of dances comprised in the whole work. To red and black were allotted fast and slow. When two or three face cards came up in succession, they referred to the possibility of duets and trios.

I played the game to find the continuity of movements for each dance, thirteen games in all. Each time a card was placed it opened up different possibilities. A card game seems to me to be a formal procedure, the rules and continuity of playing being rigorously set. But in between each game there is an informal, relaxed moment. So I made fourteen 'in-betweens'; one to begin the dance, the others to go just after each game, the last one to be the finale of the piece. These are less complex, involving repetition, and in several of them the dancers are given freedom as to where they go in the space, how often something may be done, and the possibility of exiting.

Canfield had a set by Robert Morris, a narrow vertical grey bar within which lights were fixed, that moved horizontally from one side to the other across the front of the stage, back and forth during the whole dance. The lights were fixed within the bar and moved with it, sweeping the stage slowly, spotlighting the space and the dancers.

Three Separate Elements in Time and Space

In most conventional dances there is a central idea to which everything adheres. The dance has been made to the piece of music, the music supports the dance, and the decor frames it. The central idea is emphasised by each of the several arts. What we have done in our work is to bring together three separate elements in time and space, the music, the dance and the decor, allowing each one to remain independent. The three arts don't come from a single idea which the dance illustrates, the music supports and the decor illustrates, but rather they are three separate elements each central to itself. I think it is essential now to see all the elements of theatre as both separate and interdependent. The idea of a single focus to which all adhere is no longer relevant. With the paintings of Jackson Pollock the eye can go any place on the canvas. No one point is more important than another. No point necessarily leads to another. In music, the advent of electronics also brought about a great change. The possibilities for both the sounds to be used in composing, as well as the methods of composition, were radically enlarged. Time didn't have to be measured in meter, but it could be measured in minutes and seconds, and in the case of magnetic tape in inches in space. The common denominator between music and dance is time. This brings up a new situation for dancers. If they are to involve themselves as dancers with a music measured not in beats but in actual time, how to work with it? Many choose to ignore it. I choose to see it as a necessary next step. A number of the contemporary composers were working in this not-metered way, whether they were using electronic sounds or conventional sounds. My work with John has convinced me that it was possible, even necessary for the dance to stand on its own legs rather than on the music, and also that the two arts could exist together using the same amount of time, each in its own way, one for the eye and the kinesthetic sense, the other for the ear.

Canfield, *1969, photos*
James Klosty

23

John Cage, photo James Klosty

JOHN CAGE

ROLYWHOLYOVER   A CIRCUS
by Julie Lazar

*T*he following text, adapted from a telephone
interview with Julie Lazar, Curator at The
Museum of Contemporary Art in Los
Angeles (MOCA),[1] tells the story of Rolywholyover
A Circus by John Cage, one of the composer's final
projects. Lazar worked closely with Cage on every
stage of the Circus, and has kept the project going
since his death in 1992, making every decision on
the basis of the many conversations which she had
with the composer and the spirit in which he worked.
As she looks back on the process, she recalls the
many ways in which Cage applied chance to the
Circus, the comments which he made about the art
that he loved, the humour that accompanied
whatever he did, and the willingness that he
showed, throughout his life, to try new things, to
encourage change and inquiry, and to consider
everything, from the placement of works in the
gallery spaces, to the choice of a box for the Circus
publication. 'He particularly liked the box,' Lazar
recalls, 'because he could put cookies in it!'

Rolywholyover   A Circus opened at MOCA on 12
September 1993. Its travels over the next two years
will take it to museums in the United States and
Japan, including The Menil Collection in Houston,
the Solomon R Guggenheim Museum in New York
City, the Philadelphia Museum of Art and the Art
Tower Mito Contemporary Art Center in Japan. 'In
each place,' Lazar explains, 'the Circus will take on
a different character.' And, as Cage declared, no
two days will be the same.

The development of *Rolywholyover* was definitely a
process and this process will go on until we stop
circulating the *Circus*. I originally approached John
about doing a permanently changing installation for
MOCA and he was entertained by the idea but he
didn't take me up on it. I was familiar with his work
and had met him, but our first meeting to discuss an
artist's project in greater depth was not until early
1990. He told me then that maybe we could do an
exhibition of circles. I was sitting there with big
circular earrings on and I thought he was joking! I
knew he had a good sense of humour. Of course as
we proceeded with our discussions and as I was
researching the project, I realised that he was
extremely serious. Circles play a very big part in some
of his scores and watercolours, in Jasper Johns's
Targets and in some of the *enso* scrolls which are in
the exhibition. As Cage noted, from *The Art of Zen*:
 Experts tell us that the circle has been seen as

the all, the void, and enlightenment itself . . .
[painting circles] becomes a form of activity that
continues through time . . . The monk-artist has
merely begun a process that is reactivated when
the painting is seen . . . Because the viewer has a
vital role in completing the work in his or her spirit,
true Zenga embodies the actual experience
(rather than merely the influence) of Zen. [2]
I don't recall whether in our first meeting we dis-
cussed the idea of following the course of his life as
the basis of an exhibition. I know we talked about
how it would be a non-linear, non-chronological
project. I remember talking to him about how the
audience could come in and alight on various
subjects, like bees gathering pollen, collecting their
own information about the course of his life and his
interests. It would be a kind of discovery for visitors.

He suggested that I draw up a list of art works that
I thought should be in the show. He also asked me to
obtain lists of the permanent collections in all the
modern museums in the States, which I knew was
not possible! So I suggested that we only write to the
ten museums which would have the largest holdings
of modern art. I remember at the time wondering
whether he was just going to see which collections
had holdings by the artists he admired. I didn't know
what he was going to do. I believe he wanted to
perform chance operations on the lists from those
collections but he never did because he got involved in the process we were working on, which
took on a different shape. In the end, however, we
did get some loans from those collections. John was
very familiar with visual art, many of his friends were
artists and he had 'curated' shows in the past, on
Klee, Graves, Jawlensky and Kandinsky; but he was
not really familiar with the workings of art museums.
So this project tinkers a lot with the ways in which
museums operate. It raises questions about owner-
ship, scholarship and installation, about what you
see and what you don't see. It's just like the questions of sound in Cage's compositions.

I returned to Los Angeles, read all of his books,
and later got a call from someone who was working
on a biography of Cage and had borrowed 30 years
of John's correspondence. I reviewed some of these
letters and asked John if I could borrow them. I
noted down the works and artists he had mentioned
and took this list to our next meeting. Cage had also
made a list of artists whom he thought should be in
the show. My list was unbelievable, it had several
hundred names on it; not just visual artists, but

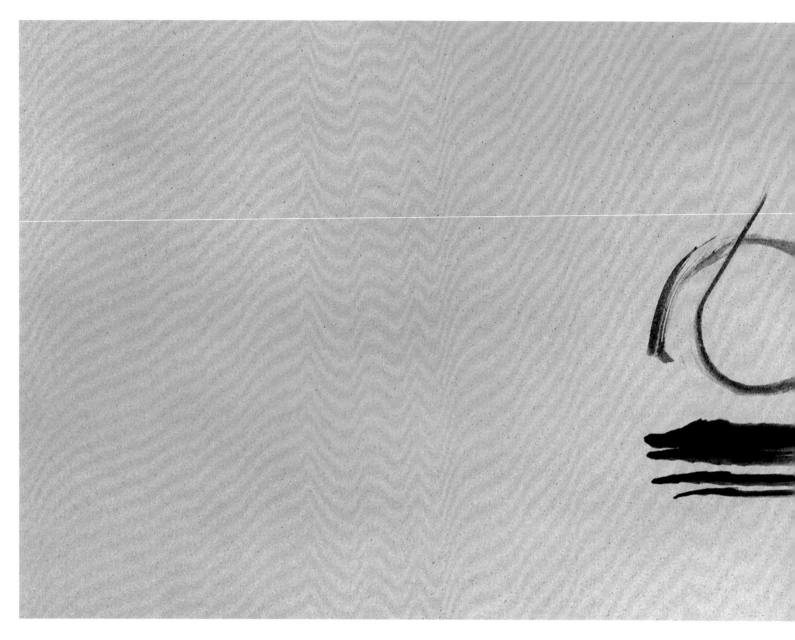

writers, composers, performers and philosophers. It's my belief that to do a show about John's life you have to touch upon all these disciplines. He eliminated a lot of people because he was trying to simplify the list so that he could perform chance operations on it.

Around this time I asked him what this project was going to be, and he quickly said that it was going to be a circus; he saw it as an opportunity for all these simultaneous presentations of different disciplines to take place. This was in keeping with previous circuses that he had done, such as the happening at Black Mountain College (1952) where simultaneous but independent actions were performed by Merce Cunningham, Robert Rauschenberg, John Cage, MC Richards, Charles Olsen and by others; his *Musicircus* (1967) with different types of simultaneous music happenings in a large space; *HPSCHD* (1967-69); and *Roaratorio* (1979) which was based on *Finnegans Wake* which John did for radio.

Then I asked him what to call this circus. While he was thinking about it I started to laugh because I

had this word in my mind from *Finnegans Wake*, which I thought was appropriate because it meant revolution and change. So I said it to him, 'rolywholyover',[3] and he laughed and wanted to know what page it was on. I actually had it in my research notes because I was reading books that were important to Cage at the time. He got a copy of the book and read the page[4] – he almost sang the page – and then he said, 'That's it!' Only later did we come to realise just how appropriate the word was because there's circularity, not only in 'rolywholyover' but in the book itself; there's circularity in the fact that John was born in Los Angeles and this, one of his last projects, originated in Los Angeles. Also the word comes after the last thunderclap in *Finnegans Wake*, and each of the thunderclaps has to do with a history of civilisation's technology. Then I found out that he had used the word in a number of writings; for example in 'writing through' *Finnegans Wake* he used it in *Roaratorio*. So it had already interested him, though I didn't know this at the time.

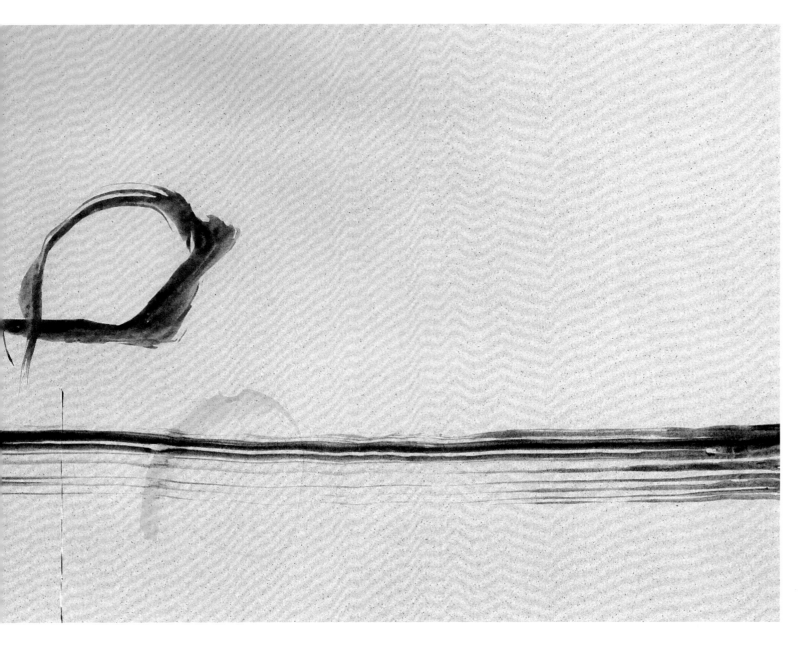

After we had agreed on the artists, I did some more research and later came to him with photographs of works which I guessed he might be interested in; works by artists whom he had written about, like Johns and Rauschenberg, or admired greatly, like Mark Tobey or Morris Graves. He had very specific ideas in mind: for instance he wanted to have 'the box with the string' by Rauschenberg – Untitled (elemental sculpture) – and a Tobey that he had once owned. I began to see that all these artists had had some kind of influence on his work. We went through the works and he would say, 'Yes, let's ask for that,' or 'No, let's not ask for that,' or 'Yes, but let's look for a later one in the series,' or 'Well, I'm more interested in the earlier Mondrians with the blue,' and so on. He really directed me. Sometimes they were works that he just loved by chance or had seen at some point in his life. We had a list of first requests and then, knowing that we weren't going to succeed in getting all of these loans, we made a second list. The third possibility was for me to find another work or to include photographic reproduc-

tions in the show.

At that time we were still operating with the idea that John was going to perform chance operations on the works which we were borrowing, to determine which ones would finally go into the Circus. Chance was going to play a large part in the process anyway, in terms of who would be willing to make the loans. Then he changed his mind and decided that he would use chance to determine the placement of the art in the galleries and the length of time that the works would be on display. That was a very important change. So the selection came about through research, through chance, through John's requests and then, since his death, when we have not been able to obtain the first or second choices, I have tried to find works that are consistent with the spirit of what John wanted.

He was not interested in figurative art, which isn't surprising; nor in some types of conceptual work that are self-concerned; nor in works in which the visual plane itself has a dominating centre of attraction. The works he chose have a lot in com-

New River Watercolour
Series II (#3), *1988,*
watercolour on paper,
66 x 182.9 cm

27

AO ANY PITCH AREA HAVING AT LEAST 20 CHROMATIC TONES. SINCE VERTICALLY · FREQUENCY, HORIZONTALLY · TIME. HORIZONTAL LINES · DURATION OF SINGLE TONES. VERTICAL LINES · CLUSTERS OR LEAST. POINTS · SHORT SINGLE TONES.

AP LINES GIVE DURATION. NOTES EQUAL STACCATO.

AQ LIKE Y, BUT USE IN EACH AREA OR IF NOTATURES ABOVE OR BELOW DOTTED LINE.

AR PLAY IN ANY WAY THAT IS SUGGESTED BY THE DRAWING.

AS A SINGLE NOTE.

AT PERFORM AS IN AE.

AU AS IN G, BUT EACH LINE MEANS ITS ONE CLEF SIGN. BRING ABOUT PITCH AMBIGUITY OF SOME OF THE INTER-SECTION NOTES.

AV AS WITH THE ADDITION OF MAKING SIGNS AMPLITUDE (1-64 ♯♯ OR ♯♯♯ ♭).

AW SEE AD.

AX NOISES OF ANY AMPLITUDE. BORDERS GIVEN. ON LINES BETWEEN AREAS · 3 BORDERS.

AY GRAIN MUSIC. NO INCH SQUARED TIME UNIT. NUMBERS WITHIN ARE OF TONES THAT MAY COMPLETE THEIR APPEARANCE WITHIN ANY AMOUNT OF THE AREA, GIVEN THEM BY GRAPH. USE TICAL GRAPH IS FREQUENCY, THE TREBLE AND BASS AREAS · MOBILE AS INDICATED.

AZ NUMBERS INDICATE TIME (ANY UNITS). NOTES CONNECTED BY LINES, VERTICAL, ARE CLUSTERS.

BA NUMBERS AS IN T. SOURCES OF NOISE AS IN AG.

BB NOTES ARE SINGLE SOUNDS. LINES ARE DURATION (D) · FREQUENCY (F), OVERTONE STRUCTURE (S), AMPLITUDE (A), AND OCCURRENCE (SUCCESSION (O). PROXIMITY TO THESE, MEASURED BY DROPPING PERPENDICULARS FROM NOTES TO LINES, GIVES, RESPECTIVELY, LONGEST, LOWEST, SIMPLEST, LOUDEST, AND EARLIEST.

BC PLAY NUMBERS OF TONES IN PITCH AREAS GIVEN. X · ANY NUMBER.

BD NOTES WITH AMPLITUDE GIVEN. ADJACENT AREAS MAY BE USED TO AFFECT ATTACK.

BE NUMBERS · EVENTS TO BE EXPRESSED. NOTES REFER TO FINGERS, HANDS, FOREARMS TO BE USED IN PLAYING.

BF NOTES CONNECTED BY LINES TONE PLAYED LEGATO. SINGLE NOTE · STACCATO. MAKE SUPERIMPOSITIONS AS SUGGESTED BY NOTATIONS.

BG INTERVALS WITH FREE APPROACHING DEPARTURES AND SOMETIMES TIES. NUMBERS INDICATE NUMBER OF TONES TO BE PLAYED WITHIN RANGE NOTATED.

BH LIKE A, BUT WITH AMBIGUOUS CLEF.

BI USE 1 OR 2 NUMBERS FOLLOWED IF 1 OR 2 NUMBERS, THE FIRST · FREQUENCIES, THE SECOND, TIME UNITS CONTINUE OR NOT.

BJ A SINGLE SOUND. BOUNDARIES ARE FREQUENCY, DURATION, AMPLITUDE, AND OVERTONE STRUCTURE. PROXIMITY AS IN BB.

BK LIKE A, BUT WITH NOTES. A, I, AND AS IN AC (AMPLITUDE FREE).

BL SINGLE NOTES ACCOMPANIED BY NUMBERS GIVING NUMBER OF TONES TO APPEAR, ABOVE, BELOW, BEFORE AND AFTER, THE ONE NOTATED.

BM FIGURES WITH AMPLITUDE GRAPHICALLY GIVEN. THE HORIZONTAL DIFFERENCE BETWEEN A PITCH AND ITS AMPLITUDE GIVES TIME AVAILABLE FOR ITONE.

BN 2 HANDS STARTING AT TWO DIFFERENT POINTS ON PERIMETER. ARRIVE EVENTUALLY AT CENTRE. TONES MAY BY ANY PATHS.

BO LIKE W WITH TIME UNITS GIVEN.

BP NUMBERS OF TONES WITHIN RANGES GIVEN FOR EACH HAND.

BQ SINGLE TONES AT ANY POINT (I. E., PITCH, DURATION) WITHIN TRIANGLES. HYPOTENUSE GIVES DYNAMICS AVAILABLE.

BR ISTHMUS/ OF TONES THAT MAY BE TAKEN IN ADVANCE FOR FRONTIERS

OF HARMONICS GIVEN ABOVE EACH AGGREGATE. PLAY AS IN B.

BS DYNAMICS AS NOTATED FOR BOTH HANDS.

BT NOTES GIVE PLACE OF PERFORMANCE WITH RESPECT TO STANTO.

BU PLAY SOUNDS GIVEN EACH NUMBER OF SOUNDS WITHIN AREAS. E. BETWEEN STAVES · SINGLE AREA, IN DELAY · TIME UNITS.

BV THREE LARGE (4 OR MORE SOUND), SIX LESS LARGE (3 SOUNDS) LO SMALL (TWO SOUND), 4 VERY SMALL POINTS (SINGLE SOUND). THE 5 LINES AND THE H BOUNDARIES TO BE USED AS IN BB AND BJ. WHERE OBTAINED MEASUREMENTS FOR 3 FREQUENCIES THE 3 DIFFERENT LINES ARE USED LIKEWISE FOR OTHER MEASUREMENTS.

BW 4 SIDED FIGURES GIVE FREQUENCY, AMPLITUDE, DURATION AND OVERTONE STRUCTURE. THE ILLUSION OF PERSPECTIVE GIVES OCCURRENCE, CLOSEST TO THE OBSERVER · EARLIEST IN TIME.

BX ALL AT ONCE LIKE A MOMENT OF A PLANT.

BY ANY NOISES, THEIR RELATIVE PITCH GIVEN GRAPHICALLY (UP HIGH, DOWN · LOW).

BZ THE 3 PEDALS WITH 1 · INACTIVITY, AND A · ACTIVITY. ANY ON NO KEYBOARD, HARP OR NOISE SOUNDS.

CA KEYBOARD (WHITE), MUTE (VERTICAL LINES), PIZZ. (BRACKETTED BY DOTTED LINES, AND FRICTION (HORIZONTAL LINES) AREAS GIVEN. NOTES OF ANY KIND WHEN AREAS OVERLAP, EITHER, BOTH BEING THUMBED MAY BE PRODUCED.

CB NUMBERS OF TONES IN PITCH AREAS GIVEN.

CC THE FOUR DIFFERENTLY DRAWN LINES · FREQUENCY, DURATION, AMPLITUDE AND TONE STRUCTURE, IN ANY CORRESPONDANCE MEASUREMENTS DEFINED THESE ARE TO DRAW PERPENDICULARLY FROM STRAIGHT LINES ABOVE OR BELOW TO THESE POINTS OF INTERSECTIONS. WITH SLANTING LINES, NUMBERS AT ENDS OF THESE GIVE BY THEIR DIFFERENCE TIME AVAILABLE FOR SOUNDS.

CD FOR · USE 1 OF 4 READINGS. FOR C · USE 2 OF 4 READINGS. FOR X · USE 3 OF

4 READINGS. HORIZONTAL READINGS · NUMBER, VERTICAL READINGS · TONER

CE CLEFS AMBIGUOUS. LEGER LINES ABOVE 9 · 15, BELOW ♯ · 13. MAKE INTERVALS AND AGGREGATES LOOSE SUGGESTED BY NOTATION.

CF AS IN BL.

3/27/58.

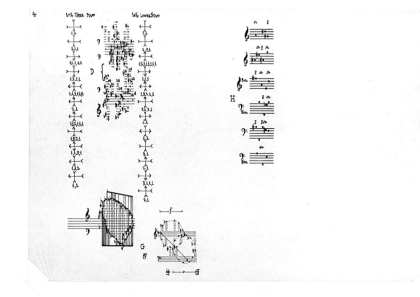

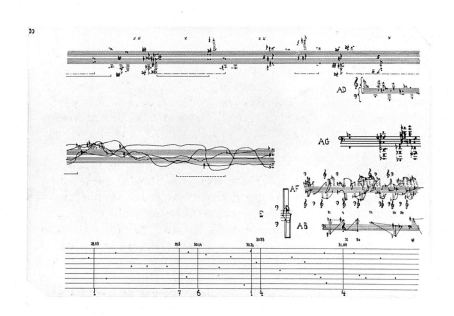

mon, even if they are by very uncommon artists. In the case of Joseph Cornell, he wanted a sand box because he liked the fact that it could change. He was also very attracted to works that had an intentional *living* quality, for example where a chemical had been applied, or works like the dirt painting that Rauschenberg had given him years before (which we don't have in this show because it's too sensitive to travel). He used to talk about this dirt painting in terms of being able to tell the change in the weather by watching how the work changed. We have a more recent clay painting by Rauschenberg in the *Circus*. He had comments to make about every artist, but they were not the kind of comments that an art historian would make. Otherwise, he never justified his choices. For example, he didn't talk about the silence or the whiteness of Robert Ryman's paintings. What he did say about Ryman was that he loved almost anything he has done. He particularly liked the work on linen and he loved the *Surface Veils*. I don't think he particularly liked the paintings that had Ryman's name on them, or any of the ones with the metal hinges or fasteners. Still, if we had only been able to obtain those, he would have been quite happy. I did ask him, thinking of Duchamp, whether there was one work that he felt *must* be in the *Circus*, and of course the answer was no, there wasn't, and that was that! With regard to Duchamp, who was one of his favourite people, he assured me that anything by him would be of interest. I think this is going to be one of the hardest and most frustrating things for critics and particularly for art historians. He was very serious about the art, he studied the work and definitely had feelings about it. But I don't now want to start analysing his choices, because *Rolywholyover   A Circus* is not just about the works that were selected; it's also about the on-going process that is involved.

Before his death, John really took the opportunity to put into motion his ideas about every aspect of the process. It's my belief that had he lived, he would have continued to shape the *Circus*. It's also my belief that because of his involvement in every aspect, he finished what he needed to get done for it to be *his* project. But I know that he would have continued to refine it throughout the course of the show. He set some kind of framework for everything. He met with everyone who would be instrumental to the project, including the composer Andrew Culver, who had performed chance operations before with John, and who he is performing the chance operations for *Rolywholyover* using Cage's computerised process.

Once John had decided to make the main gallery space into a composition and that chance was going to determine the placement and duration of the works, he returned to the idea of using chance to determine the content of the other installations. He had tried this before in a museum in Germany and loved it. It basically becomes like a collage of permanent collections that he named *Museumcircle*. He instructed me to write to all the

museums in Los Angeles, but I suggested that we just write to those within a 30-mile radius. So we wrote to 130 museums and 21 responded. The question was, 'What ten objects would you be willing to loan for a project by John Cage?' Some museums decided to do chance operations on their permanent collections, some chose works which they thought related to Cage.

All the 21 correspondences went to John and he performed chance operations on them; that is he asked the computer to give him numbers from one to ten and it gave him something like 644 numbers. We then sent him the list of works and he went through the chart, doing chance operations. If the first number was four, for example, he would take the first document and select the fourth object. The works selected by chance include *French Peep Show Box*, *c*1820, from the California Museum of Science and Industry; *Small Elephant Seal Skull* from the Cabrillo Marine Museum; and *Ingrid Bergman's Bustier from the film 'Cactus Flower'* from Frederick's of Hollywood Lingerie Museum. We are also using chance to install the works by pulling numbers out of a hat! John also wanted to have some books in this space, about the artists, composers, writers, etc, who are in the show or who interested him. There are tables where people can read these books and also play chess; and there are potted trees and river rocks; all in that one space. He wanted it to be an unoppressive space where people would feel they could actually live. John didn't have a lot of things in his loft in New York. In the place where most people worked with him there was a round table with several chairs, surrounded by plants, surrounded by art, surrounded by the noises of 6th Avenue. It was very minimal. So all this is in the first gallery.

We were still in the process of working on the next gallery when he died. It's an installation of his works. He wanted me to choose his visual art works and performances, though had he lived, I would have tried to get his involvement in this too. In the adjoining space there is an installation of his prints, watercolours and musical scores, installed by chance. John and I were together in Barcelona for an exhibition of his graphic works, and the curator asked him if he would do the installation himself. So he walked through the space, counting out the approximate measurements in feet, then he numbered each work and put the numbers into two 'hats' (a nod to Duchamp and the manner in which he composed *Erratum Musical*), which were actually an empty trash can and a plastic bag! In one he put the space designation, in the other the work designation. Then he shuffled his hands into both 'hats' and pulled out numbers. In this way he matched a space and a work. If any of the works collided he used choice to separate them a little; but for the most part they stayed where chance had determined they would be. We are following the same idea for this installation. John was very clear that he didn't want

OPPOSITE: 'Solo for Piano', from Concert for Piano and Orchestra, *1957-58, 63 pages, ink on paper, each page 28 x 42.8 cm, Northwestern University Music Library, John Cage 'Notations' Collection, ABOVE: An introductory page; CENTRE: Page 4; BELOW: Page 20; photos Prudence Cuming Associates*

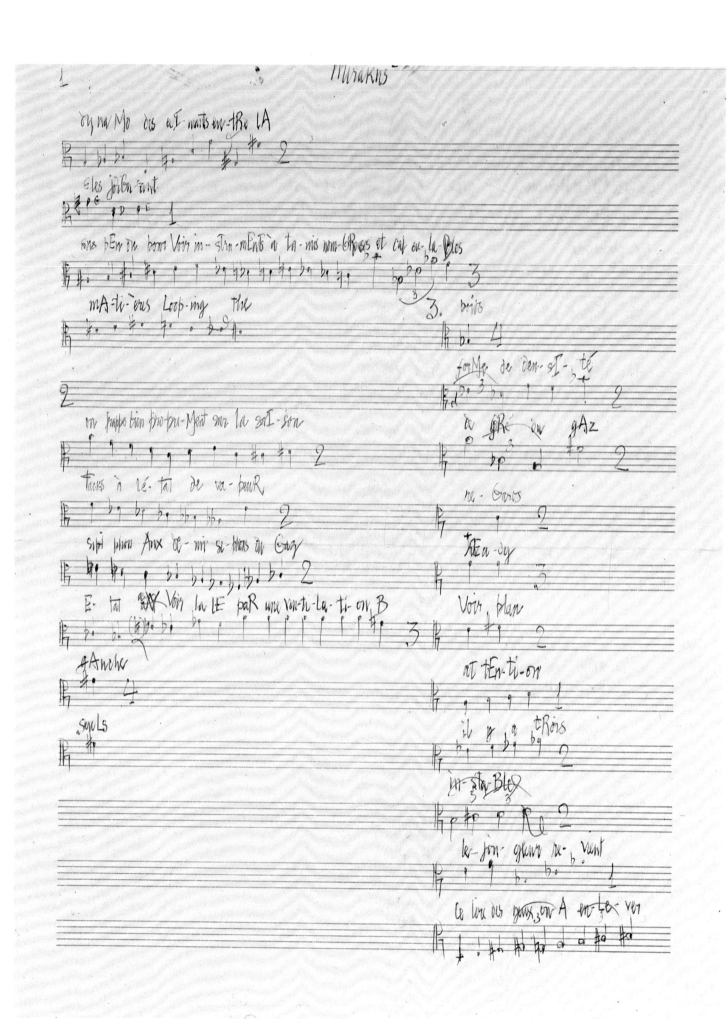

Mirakus[2], *1985, worksheet with notations, photo David Sundberg*

ABOVE: New River Watercolour Series IV (#7)*, 1988, watercolour on paper, 60 x 101.6 cm; BELOW:* Where R = Ryoanji R/16 – 3/
90*, 1990, pencils on handmade Japan paper, 25.4 x 48.3 cm*

to be the centre of the show himself, even though we were roughly following the course of his life. But I think he understood my reason for wanting this gallery. There aren't many opportunities for people to come into contact with his visual art. He was coming round to the idea, but he didn't initiate it.

In the main gallery there are movable walls. The main requirement for this space was that everything should have the ability to move and that the natural or artificial light should be as unobtrusive as possible, so there would not be any focusing. John did not like seeing works of art in linear placement, at eye level. So the positioning of works is going to be determined by chance. He also didn't like linearity with the placement of scores. So we came up with the idea of having translucent flat files, which in a way refer to his *plexigrams* which were called *Not wanting to say anything about Marcel.* Our flat files are translucent and there is UV protection on the top of the drawers when you pull them out, to protect the documents and objects which appear to float in space. Chance will also determine in which drawers the documents and objects are placed. It becomes almost like an interactive sculptural environment. This idea pleased John very much.

There is also an installation containing the *enso* scrolls and this is where he returns to the idea of circles. Some are authentic Japanese *enso* scrolls, others are like found *ensos* where a pot that was used for cooking rice was put down on a piece of paper and a circle was burned into it. These are going to be installed in a circular installation that moves. The ability of the audience to view them is determined by chance. There will be an art handler following Cage's score who will come in and roll up a curtain or roll it down according to the chance determinations. The translucent flat files will also be moved about in the space according to chance, and the position of the movable walls will be determined by chance.

There are different designations for the movement of works and this is to contend with problems of fragility. Any work that is very fragile and cannot be moved about will be brought into the gallery by chance and be placed on a permanent wall, and will then be removed from the gallery wall by chance and be placed in a reservoir within the space, not to return. The next designation has to do with works that are still fragile but can be moved for viewing within the space on a movable wall. The last designation is for works that are very stable and can therefore go anywhere on the movable walls or on the stationary walls.

There is a movable interactive sound studio by David Rosenboom. John, David and I had talked about how to include other composers in the show and John was disinclined to have a scheduled space for listening. He didn't like recordings anyway unless he was using them for source material. David Rosenboom is a composer who is Dean of the School of Music at Cal Arts where he has an experimental laboratory. He suggested doing an installation where the visitor could combine the music of different composers, for example a David Tudor composition with a Cage composition

with something by Erik Satie. In that way audiences actually experience the chance operations. John liked that idea very much. It's just one computer with four headphones so the music will not be heard in the gallery, again according to John's instructions. Many people were expecting performances of the music with the works of art, but John wanted only the ambient sounds. The other interactive computer installation is by Jim Rosenberg who helped John to develop some of his computer programmes, most notably the programme for the creation of poetry called *mesostics*. His piece is called *Intergrams* and visitors will be able to make their own poetry from a library of text compiled by Rosenberg. The position of these computers will move according to chance.

The last space is the auditorium and John instructed that there should always be something going on. It could be empty so that people could just listen to silence. Or they could be listening to Satie's *Vexations*, or they could be watching Nam June Paik's *Zen for Film*, or seeing a performance. John said that the announcement of whatever was going to happen in that space should be given only on the day of the event; so people would not be able to find out on what day they could see David Tudor or Merce Cunningham; they would just have to come and see what was there. There will be all kinds of things going on. One is that on three different days during the three months a number of people will take part in something called 'Cage + Questions We Ask.' Each participant will prepare three questions and three statements. These will be mixed up and pulled from a hat and the group will discuss whichever question and answer has come out of the hat. The audience is also encouraged to leave questions in the gallery or to mail them in advance. There are concerts by many artists, many of whom worked with Cage. It will not only be Cage's music. There are readings, film screenings and John's radio compositions. John also instructed that the events be scheduled within a time bracket, so if we have a 60-minute film, for example, it will be announced to take place within a 90-minute time frame. The idea behind this is that any time is a good time, and that if you get there and find something unexpected, then you have to make something of it.

We have all had to change the way we do things. For example, the art handlers have become visible and part of the choreography of chance. This fits in very well with John's belief that art is social action. In his 1967 *Diary: How to Improve the World (You Will Only Make Matters Worse)*, for example, he submitted that, 'Art, instead of being an object made by one person is a process set in motion by a group of people. Art's socialised. It isn't someone saying something, but people doing things, giving everyone (including those involved) the opportunity to have experiences they would not otherwise have had.'[5] The score used in the gallery for changing works provides for a lot of flexibility. There are going to be about three time brackets each day for the art handlers to follow. One day, for example, chance may have determined that six works be moved between the hours of 11 and noon; and 12 between the hours of noon and three; and so on. It's up to the art handlers whether they move the works quickly, or whether they take their time; also if the work is large, then that situation will determine how long it will take to move. They just have to begin their work before a certain time and end it before a certain time which is indicated on the score. John said that no two days of *Rolywholyover* would be the same.

The impact of the *Circus* started a long time ago for us and a lot of people have already been involved in the process. When it opens to the public it becomes larger, and when the critics start to write about it it becomes even larger, so who knows what will happen! This *Circus* has a life of its own. We don't know how things will change. I've already noticed that people who were resisting it at first are now becoming creatively involved. I think that would have pleased Cage very much. Every city that the *Circus* travels to, every viewer who sees it, will have a different response.

The *Citycircus* was not John's idea. I realised that at the point in Cage's career when we began working, people would be expecting a retrospective, including an in-depth study on his work with Merce Cunningham; but Cage was developing a new project so we didn't have the opportunity to do that at MOCA. So I called together a number of organisations, and asked them whether they were interested in addressing any of the items in the show in greater depth. The ideas came from them. There are about 30 organisations involved, including the Los Angeles Children's Museum, the Los Angeles Philharmonic Association, Beyond Baroque Literary/Arts Center, the Center Theatre Group/Mark Taper Forum, Claremont Colleges, and Electronic Café International. There's a great diversity. I know there have been similar meetings in New York, Philadelphia and Houston, but in each place on the tour,

Rolywholyover   A Circus will take on a different character.

As far as the publication is concerned, we worked on a regular catalogue for quite a long time. Then John changed his mind. He just wanted to have a box with diverse things in it. He wanted a lot of the material to be free in the gallery and then sold together in the box. I think it was an affectionate tribute to Duchamp, although he never said so. I drew up a list of texts that he had claimed had been important to him and we started making some choices. But we made so many choices that we couldn't have all of those things in the publication! I asked him what of his work should be in the box and I sent him a list of the titles and chapters and pages, and he did chance operations on them. There were something like 180 pages just of that! Before he died, he worked on everything that we were intending to choose from, so there was nothing in it that he hadn't wanted. He had met with the graphic designer and MOCA's editor and said that he wanted the publication to be clear, to have lots of material, to be confusing and to feel as if nothing had really been done. And he wanted us to understand that all of the material is equal. He chose the paper and also the box. He particularly liked the box because he could put cookies in it! In fact after he died, I came to be with Merce in New York and one evening we sat down and finished the cookies which were in John's prototype box. So in the box there will be the recipe for those cookies. There will be some scores and some reproductions of works of art from John's original list. Some art works not in the show will have some visual representation in the box. I don't know if it's going to be as confusing as he wanted it to be; it might even be prettier than he would have liked! But I think we managed to maintain his spirit. We'll never know. But I believe we did.

Notes

1 This interview was conducted by Clare Farrow on 23 July 1993.
2 Stephen Addiss, *The Art of Zen: Paintings and Calligraphy by Japanese Monks, 1600-1925*, Abrams, New York, 1989, p6.
3 I first encountered 'rolywholyover' in Norman O Brown's *Closing Time*, Vintage, New York, 1974, p36.
4 James Joyce, *Finnegans Wake*, Viking Press, New York, 1939, p597.
5 John Cage, *A Year From Monday*, Wesleyan University Press, Middletown, Connecticut, 1969, p151.

John Cage during Mountain Lake Workshop, 1988, photo Stephanie Klein

River Rocks & Smoke 4/10/90 (#21), *1990, watercolour on paper prepared with smoke, 182.9 x 121.3 cm*

JOHN CAGE
PAYING ATTENTION
by Anne d'Harnoncourt

While the ordinary non-artistic experiences of sight afford so much material for plastic art that the vulgar conception of good painting is that it is deceptively like nature, the ordinary non-artistic experience of sound has so little in common with music that musical realism is, with rare though popular exceptions, generally regarded as an eccentricity. [1] Encyclopedia Britannica

I work in many ways in a given time period. And not only do I make music, but I write texts and now I make etchings. I do all of these things in different ways. Some ideas that I have I drop, and others I pick up from the past and so on. So it's not a linear situation. It's more like overlapping layers. [2] John Cage

I began doing graphic notations, and those graphic notations led other people to invite me to make graphic works apart from music. And those led me in turn to make musical scores that were even more graphic . . . I don't feel that I'm being unfaithful to music when I'm drawing. [3] Cage

I try to discover what one needs to do in art by observations from my daily life. I think daily life is excellent and that art introduces us to it and to its excellences the more it begins to be like it. [4] Cage

I think everyone would benefit from drawing. [5] Cage

We must arrange our music, we must arrange our Art, we must arrange everything, I believe, so that people realise that they themselves are doing it, and not that something is being done to them. [6] Cage

When trying to write something about John Cage, where should one be? There is no 'should' and there is everywhere – a street corner in Manhattan would be excellent, or deep woods or a train crossing India (or Kansas). Cage's lifelong openness to the visual world puts the rest of us to thinking hard about how we see as well as hear. Perhaps his most important conviction for us to understand is that the world is full of wonderful things, each of which has its individual colour, texture, sound, weight, scale, duration, shape, density, and which, if left alone, comes to our attention with its own character intact. John Cage was a delight to observe observing. Surveying the ground as he walked in a wet field, he found mushrooms; listening to a roomful of silence, he heard his blood circulate in his veins; concentrating on a game of chess, he enjoyed a nearby waterfall. What is amazing in his work is the confluence of attentiveness to the details of daily life with a joyful, sometimes daunting, discipline.

To talk about Cage as a visual artist is to seek the visual in all of his work. One might start with that entirely characteristic handwriting in which his music, letters, texts, mesostics, prints and drawings were made – a sign of himself that is never submerged and remains spare, meticulous, finely drawn, with an increasing tendency toward the curve and the loop. For the layman, not knowing the mysteries (or the clarities) of moving music from the human mind to paper, it is difficult to express one's reaction to the visual quality of Cage's scores. Sometimes they are infinitely beautiful in craft, invention and deliberation, as in the case of *Concert for Piano and Orchestra* (1957-58) in which he used 'eighty-four varieties of compositional technique, each giving rise to a more or less distinctive graphic style.'[7] Sometimes they consist of jotted notes and instructions, as in *WGBH-TV* (1971) and *Child of Tree* (1975). The compressed force and serenity, freedom and control of a Japanese Haiku poem offers one analogy – the vast musical landscape of Mozart or the journals of Thoreau, threaded with tiny drawings of things seen on walks in nature, provide others. While early compositions had mingled visual and musical ideas (*Chess Pieces*, *c*1944, for example),[8] *Water Music* of 1952 was among the first of Cage's scores in which he deliberately emphasised its visual nature. Inscribed in India ink on large sheets in a bold, quirky but elegant hand, the score was to be mounted like a poster during the performance, visible to both performer and audience.

What is to be said about Cage's personal taste for the visual work of others (Klee, Tobey, Graves, Lippold, Rauschenberg, Johns) and its relationship to his own setting of pen or burin or broad brush to paper? A clear preference for delicacy of execution with no shyness about intensity – declared fondness for an element of mystery. We recall that throughout his life he composed pieces for great virtuosos (David Tudor, Cathy Berberian, Grete Sultan, Paul Zukofsky) whose passion for exploring the possibilities of their instrument (or voice) led composer and performer together towards marvellously difficult music. While the *ego* is put aside, the individual eye, ear and hand were never discouraged. He had a taste for simplicity and a taste for complexity. A love of Zen gardens, a love of Times Square at dusk. Everything and nothing. It is not surprising that etching became Cage's favourite medium in printmaking, which he approached as a new adventure in 1978: difficult to master, precise and beautiful in its line, capable of infinite detail. The lithograph may have seemed too dramatic to Cage – he later let fire and smoke themselves bring drama to the printer's table. But he loved choosing paper, and strongly favoured blue in an infinitude of shades. He remarked to the printers working with him in 1979-82 that he wanted his colours 'to look like they went to graduate school.'[9]

The interpenetration, coexistence of things: Cage's edible drawings. You can look at them, you can eat them, no waste. Cooking was as much a part of Cage's life as composing music, poetry, or prints – isn't cooking all about mixture and letting individual flavours hold our attention? Cage's scores for music, scores for prints, recipes for chicken, all exist for realisation by the artist in real time, and he invited his audience (or his dinner guests) to realise that listening, looking, and eating are also creative acts. We remember his story about the pleasure of eating and conversing in a restaurant with swimmers diving outside the window and a jukebox playing.[10]

The question of scale enters as an ingredient. At one pole: *4'33"* in 1952 with one piano and one performer in a room of surprised silence and sound. At the other: *HPSCHD* in 1969 with seven harpsichords, 208 tapes, 58 channels of amplified sound, NASA films of space travel, 6,400 slides from eight projectors on a 340-foot circular screen, and an audience of 6,000, lasting four and a half hours. They are both music, and they are surely also both spectacle. A purposeful joining of sight and sound experienced in real time and space – recordings are useless, because being there is all important, *seeing* and *hearing* together. The theatre is after all where multiple arts and artists coincide – the written, sung, and spoken word, the actor, the dancer, the musician, the set designer, the prop and the costume, the gesture and the music. Cage seems to have loved theatre in that sense always. ('[Theatre] simply means the use of all one's senses.'[11]) Simultaneous performances of Cage's music and Merce Cunningham's dance share time and space, share our attention, share the invisible field inhabited by sounds and the visible field occupied by the musicians, the dancers, and ourselves. Theatre as the layering of the visual and aural so that the audience does the mixing.

The *Europeras* (1987) were among Cage's most witty and lighthearted *gesamtkunstwerke* in which sounds and sights combined. He saw them as three-dimensional and aural collages. Having steered clear of opera all his life as overly expressive in every way, Cage found himself intrigued by the unfolding possibilities of combining snatches of arias, familiar costumes for singers performing unfamiliar roles, lighting and props set free by chance operations to function as independent agents.

Is there a fear of being too beautiful? A dilemma for Duchamp, but Cage saw beauty everywhere. The snow shovel chosen from a hardware store out of indifference; a stone chosen from a river bed loved for itself. Each thing taken on its own terms, not for its

references to other things. Cage's music often generated delicious lists of specific 'things' which are to be seen, moved, struck. 'Beer bottles, flower pots, cowbells, automobile brake drums, dinner bells, thunder sheets, and in the words of Mr Cage, "anything we can lay our hands on",' wrote a bedazzled critic in 1942 apropos of a percussion performance in Chicago.[12] 43 years later we find Cage carefully heating up a little iron Japanese teapot to make circular impressions on a monotype. One thinks of all his instruments as beautiful: the piano prepared, the cactus amplified by a cartridge, a great conch shell filled with water.

Cage's scores are as varied as the sounds to which they give rise: *Seven Haiku* (1952) with conventional notation for these brief piano pieces as beautifully and sparely inked as their namesake poems are written; transparent overlays of mylar printed with ameboid forms and dotted lines for *Cartridge Music* (1960); the voluminous *Songbooks* (1970) with Marcel Duchamp's severe Norman profile or a map of Concord serving as melodic lines to be sung; *Renga* (1976), which incorporates 361 drawings by Thoreau. Whether Cage used his own inimitable variations on conventional notation or dived happily into what he called 'graphism' (particularly during the 1960s), he seems always to have seen the writing out of a score as inextricable from its character, whether established by choice or chance. 'I don't hear music when I write it. I write in order to hear something I haven't yet heard. My writing is almost characterised by having something unusual in the notation. The notation is about something that is not familiar.'[13]

As Cage's notion of notation grew freer, musicians were asked to play scores which he (or they) derived from flaws in a sheet of paper (*Music for Piano*, 1955), star charts (*Atlas Eclipticalis*, 1961, *Etudes Australes*, 1970), and knots in a piece of plywood (*Music for Carillon V*, 1967). Colour entered early on – the singer of *Aria* (1958) takes her cue from red, yellow, blue, or green hand-coloured lines which skip, dive, and undulate across the page like inebriated caterpillars, each of ten colours standing for a style of singing. It is amusing to recall (did Cage?) that the staff in European music notation began in the tenth century with a red line for the fixed 'F' and a yellow one for 'C'.[14]

Entering a field new to him in which the work of so many of his friends and colleagues held his profound admiration, Cage approached opportunities to make what might be described as works of visual art with great modesty, but also with that same intense concentration and joyful anticipation of unexpected outcomes with which he approached musical composition. *Not Wanting to Say Anything About Marcel* in 1969 found him responding to the death of an old and revered friend whose own complex mingling of intellectual and visual ideas might have presented an impossible challenge. With the aid of a dictionary to which he applied chance operations, and in collaboration with Calvin Sumsion, Cage moved gently into a kind of concrete poetry. Letters and fragments of words float on a Plexiglas field, and he characteristically sought to maintain both multiplicity and transparency by setting eight sheets of clear plastic printed with words in stands so that the viewer peered through them; and if he wasn't careful, his gaze passed beyond them – just as the viewer finds himself contemplating the fountain in the courtyard of the Philadelphia Museum of Art when he thought he was examining Duchamp's *Large Glass.*

Almost another ten years passed before Cage took up printmaking in earnest, accepting the invitation of Kathan Brown and Tom Marioni to work at Crown Point Press in San Francisco in the same spirit of adventure that he would have accepted an elephant ride through the Himalayas.[15] Cage's prints and his scores reflect the same way of working: setting forth tasks to be accomplished, discipline to be maintained, new skills to be mastered. It seems natural that printmaking would have attracted him with its venerable (but new to him) panoply of instruments and procedures and the array of gifted 'performers' in the form of the Crown Point printers who were at hand to collaborate with him. His work over 14 years of annual sessions at the Press was an extended exploration of his own and others' ability to harvest new territory.[16] Working side by side with the printers, Cage composed the 'score' for successive images, using chance operations to make a wealth of specific determinations about colour, plate size and shape, technique, and the frequency with which any of those appeared, while the printers performed the often wildly intricate tasks of printing that which had been composed the previous day. Neither artist nor printer knew what the result would look like, just as the composer and performers of *Fontana Mix* (1958) could not 'hear' the sounds they would make before sitting down to play them. Contrary to frequent practice, Cage as printmaker remained in the workshop as the printers pulled the complete edition – indeed his presence was usually essential, as he intended changes to be made in each successive print.

Although the span of time during which Cage made prints was relatively short (he began in earnest when he was 65), he accomplished an astonishing array of work and gave no sign of having exhausted his interest or his energies in a field which proved in turn to affect his music as he grew more excited by his discoveries. Beginning in 1978 with a (figuratively) blindfolded plunge into the new medium (*Seven Day Diary, Not Knowing*), he produced small wiry images that seem resolutely Cagean in their mingling of energy and delicacy. A few months before his death, he completed *HV2* (1992), a measured and muted sequence of 15 abstract compositions in pale colours which bring us up short as being both beautiful, unexpectedly simple in appearance, and serenely elegiac. The arrangement of horizontal and vertical elements (slender rectangles of discarded copper plate) for each image was done by eye, while colour mixes were arrived at by chance operations. Between those two poles lies a wealth of work that grows more interesting as it recedes in time. It is remarkable, yet should not surprise us, that a print by John Cage looks like nothing else – it bears the same

determined conviction that marks his work as a musician and a writer in seeking to avoid 'taste' and yet being free to 'choose'; he chooses a characteristic beauty, which tends to the abstract and suggests the abundance and austerity of nature.

Two extended series of etchings, *Changes and Disappearances* (1979-82) and *On the Surface* (1980-82) carry the patient and attentive observer into related but very different realms. For *Changes*, Cage borrowed visual clues and methods from two of his mentors, Thoreau and Duchamp, and carried out an extended series of chance operations to determine the colours, position (or absence) of a mark or line on the sheet of paper, and the number of such marks on any given plate. The sequence of 35 prints rises from relative simplicity in the initial images of the series to a fabulously complex network of lines and tints (298 colours) in the final print (no 35) which seems, perhaps not surprisingly, musical in feel. Some of Cage's inspiration for this sequence must have sprung from his earlier preparation for several pieces of music of overlapping sheets of transparent materials (straight lines, biomorphic shapes, dots) from which each performer was to assemble his or her score. But the delight in delicate colour and individuality of form, the exploration of the vast amount of visual information which the relatively limited field of the sheet of paper could encompass, is also akin to the experience of watching a performance of the Cunningham Dance Company while listening simultaneously to one of Cage's relatively subdued compositions.

In *On the Surface*, Cage deliberately sought a means to achieve the 'visual equivalent of extreme quiet.'[17] With Mark Tobey's beloved 'white writing' in mind, and perhaps the Duchampian image of shards of shattered glass, Cage devised a method of making these etchings which so pleased him that he extended it to musical composition in *Thirty Pieces for Five Orchestras* of 1981. Beginning with 32 discarded scraps of copper plates found at the Press, most of which bore accidental marks or scratches, Cage cut each of them in two along curved, chance-determined lines. Using a fixed grid of 64 segments and a floating grid to be located and rotated on it, Cage arrived at the placement of each plate by consulting the *I Ching*, which also determined which plates would be used and what colour each would be. The plate fragments were to be inked and then wiped, so that each one bore a thin 'plate tone' of palest colour. In the course of printing the sequence of 35, an imaginary 'horizon line' below which the plate fragments swim, dropped by 35 equal increments until the remaining space below it coincided with the golden section of the sheet of paper. If a plate fell on the 'horizon', it was cut on a straight line at that point, so that the number of plates increased and their size decreased as they gradually fall towards the bottom of the sheets of paper, like plankton sifting downwards towards the ocean floor. The marine image is one Cage had in mind from a visit to an apparently empty tank in an aquarium, in which every now and then a clam emerged from the sand, sailed to the surface,

Mountain Lake Workshop, Cage's Big Brush and Paint Through, 1988, photo Stephanie Klein

Ryoanji is the name of the Zen Buddhist temple in Kyoto famous for its rock-and-sand garden. The notations of the flute glissandi were made by ~~drawing~~ following parts of the perimeters of stones ~~in order to~~ connecting chance determined points. The percussion accompaniment represents the raked sand.

The performance is both live and pre-recorded.

Twinning Gallery (Houst. & Prince)
568 Beroy
Jan 31   6:00

took in bubbles of air, and sank swiftly and gracefully back to invisibility. In *On the Surface* the overlapping in Cage's art of elements drawn from his experience of nature, the art of others, and his own experience as composer produced a visual purity and serenity that is profoundly contemplative.

Cage's plunge into watercolour occurred when he was 76 and accepted an invitation to join a workshop in that medium run by Ray Kass in the Appalachians at Mountain Lake, Virginia. Attracted to the large smooth black stones along the banks of the New River, he selected 15 and asked the *I Ching* for guidance as to the number of stones, the size and nature of the paper, the mix of colours, and the choice among a large number of available brushes for use in each work. The resulting images are broadly brushed, yet delicate, with the loosely defined shapes of the stones often sinking into the lower third of long sheets of horizontal or vertical paper. They recall in their awkward elegance those Japanese scrolls with ink painting or calligraphy by happily drunken poets, and the elaborate calculations behind their freshness and simplicity are difficult to guess at. A later series called *River Rocks and Smoke* (1990) came as close as any works on paper could to the incorporation of the beautiful, destructive, and ephemeral element of fire, which had fascinated Cage all of his life and the sound of which whispers and roars through *Inlets* and other late compositions. Fire and smoke appear in his Crown Point prints in many guises, beginning in 1985.

Cage never seemed to exhaust his interest in something once he discovered its attraction – the white paintings of Rauschenberg, the rocks of Ryoanji, the minute nature drawings of Thoreau remained talismans and inspirations. But his use of the same element in a score, a print or a text can change dramatically over time. The influence of the dry garden of Ryoanji first surfaces in Cage's amazing *Concert for Piano and Orchestra of* 1957-58, and resurfaces 25 years later in the drypoints *R3* and *R3* (1983), and *Where R = Ryoanji* (1983-90). He thus moved from a series of etchings to a

sequence of drawings and more etchings, and finally back to music in *Ryoanji* (1983-85): a group of superimposable compositions with graphic scores for individual instruments, in which the performer is to 'brush' the sound in and out of existence, 'as much as possible like sound events in nature rather than sounds in music.'[18]

Cage's last 15 years of music seemed to move in two directions at once, both of which are in accord with his increasing, almost overwhelming, sense of the presence of nature. On the one hand, *Roaratorio* (1979) piled sounds, words, and performers together in increasingly dense layers to produce a kind of thunder and lightning as their combined energies coincide; on the other hand, many late works for a soloist or a small number of performers let individual instruments or elements speak alone, simply or with great complexity. The prints and watercolours have their equivalent to these dual movements, if we compare the grand density for *R3* (1983), in which Cage drew 3,375 times around 15 rocks in delicate drypoint, with the quiet of the little monoprints on grey paper, *Without Horizon* (1992). Whereas earlier he had added (or multiplied) elements to make his prints more complex, in preparing plates for *Without Horizon* he gradually reduced the number of marks he intended to make from 11 to a maximum of five. Cage's twin tendencies, to multiply and to simplify, are as evident in his visual work as in his music.

Rereading the preceding words, which seem inadequate, I am flying from Philadelphia to Kansas City. As I look down at the remote, variegated surface of gently rumpled clouds stretching to the horizon under soft raking light, and up at a single aeroplane flying parallel to the one I am in, with the crisp, white line of its jet trail dissolving continually into blue nothingness, they propose themselves as useful material for a score, for a print, for contemplation, for getting on with things. As John Cage so often said, 'Marvellous'.

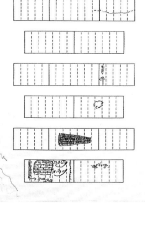

Notes

'Paying Attention' was written for *Rolywholyover   A Circus* and is contained in the box publication.

1   *Encyclopedia Britannica*, 11th ed, sv 'music'.

2   Interview with Cole Gagne and Tracy Garas, 1980, in *Conversing With Cage*, ed Richard Kostelanetz, 1989, p71.

3   Interview with EV Grimes, 1984, *ibid*, p184.

4   Interview with Michael Kirby and Richard Schechner, 1965, *ibid*, p74.

5   In conversation with Bill Anastasi (as repeated to the author, 1993).

6   Interview with Roger Reynolds, in *John Cage*, Henmar Press, New York, 1962, p47.

7   Paul Griffiths, *Cage*, Oxford Studies of Composers, Oxford University Press, Oxford, 1981, p33.

8   Illustrated in *John Cage: An Anthology*, ed Richard Kostelanetz, Da Capo Press, New York, plate 17.

9   Quoted in Kathan Brown, 'John Cage (1912-1992), Overview,' *Crown Point Press Newsletter*, (Fall 1992) p1.

10 John Cage, *A Year From Monday*, Wesleyan University

Press, 1969, p133.

11 Roger Reynolds interviewing Cage, in *John Cage*, Henmar Press, New York, 1962, p49.

12 Pence James, 'People call it Noise, but He Calls it Music,' *Chicago Daily News*, 19 March 1942, in *John Cage: An Anthology*, p61.

13 Cage in audiotape interview with Joel Eric Suben, 1983, from Richard Kostelanetz, *Conversing with Cage*, p63.

14 *Encyclopedia Britannica*, 11th ed, sv 'musical notation'.

15 See Cage statement to David Revill in *The Roaring Silence*, Arcade Publishing, New York, 1992, p261.

16 I am extremely grateful to Kathan Brown and her extraordinary staff at Crown Point Press for discussions of Cage's work there, during my visit in February 1993.

17 Revill, *The Roaring Silence*, p270. See the description of *On the Surface* by Paul Singdahlsen in *John Cage Etchings 1978-82*, Crown Point Press, San Francisco, 1982, pp22-25.

18 Revill, p279.

ABOVE: Renga, ink on vellum, 1976; OPPOSITE ABOVE: Note regarding flute part for Ryoanji, 1983-85; OPPOSITE BELOW: James Joyce, Marcel Duchamp, Erik Satie: An Alphabet, 1981, two pages from steno notebook; photos David Sundberg

THE BLOW OF THE SUBLIME
by Susan Sontag

Lincoln Kirstein, the finest historian of the dance and one of its greatest ideologues ever, has observed that in the 19th century what the prestige of ballet really amounted to was the reputation of the dancer, and that even when there were great choreographers (notably Petipa) and great dance scores (from Adam, Delibes and Tchaikovsky), dance was still almost entirely identified for the large theatrical public with the personality and virtuosity of great dancers. The triumphant mutation in dance taste and in the composition of dance audiences which occurred just before World War I, in response to the authoritative intensity and exoticism of the Ballets Russes, did not challenge the old imbalance of attention – not even with the subsequent invention by Diaghilev of dance as an ambitious collaboration in which major innovative artists outside the dance world were brought in to enhance this theatre of astonishment. The score might be by Stravinsky, the decor by Picasso, the costumes by Chanel, the libretto by Cocteau. But the blow of the sublime was delivered by Nijinsky or Karsavina – by the dancer. According to Kirstein, it was only with the advent of a choreographer so complete in his gifts as to change dance forever, George Balanchine, that the primacy of the choreographer over the performer, of dance over the dancer, finally came to be understood.

Kirstein's account of the more limited perspectives of dance publics before Balanchine is, of course, not incorrect. But I would point out that the exaltation of the performer over all else pervaded not only dance in the 19th century but all the arts that have to be performed. Recalling the effusive identification of dance with the dancer – say, with Marie Taglioni and with Fanny Elssler – one should recall as well other audiences, other raptures. The concert audiences ravished by Liszt and Paganini were also identifying music with the performer; the music was, as it were, the occasion. Those who swooned over La Malibran in the new Rossini or Donizetti thought of opera as a vehicle of the singer. (As for the *look* of the opera, whether it was the staging, the decor, or the often incongruous physique of the singer – this hardly seemed worthy of discussion.) And in recent decades the focus of attention has been modified in these arts too. Even the most diva-besotted portion of the opera public is now prepared to slice the work from the performance, vocal prowess and expressiveness from acting – making distinctions that were fused in the

inflatedly partisan rhetoric of extreme reactions (either ecstasy or the rudest condemnation) which surrounded opera performance, particularly the early performances of a new work, in the 19th century. That the work is now routinely seen as transcending the performer, rather than the performer transcending the work, has come to be felt not just in dance, because of the advent of a supremely great choreographer, but in all the performing arts.

And yet, this having been said, there seems to be something intrinsic to dance that warrants the kind of reverential attention paid in each generation to a very few dancers – something about what they do that is different from the achievements of surpassingly gifted, magnetic performers in other arts to whom we pay homage.

Dance cannot exist without dance design: choreography. But dance *is* the dancer.

The relation of dancer to choreographer is not just that of executant or performer to *auteur* – which, however creative, however inspired the performer, is still a subservient relation. Though a performer in this sense too, the dancer is also more than a performer. There is a mystery of incarnation in dance that has no analogue in the other performing arts.

A great dancer is not just performing (a role) but being (a dancer). Someone can be the greatest Odette/Odile, the greatest Albrecht one has ever seen – as a singer can be the best (in anyone's memory) Tosca or Boris or Carmen or Sieglinde or Don Giovanni, or an actor can be the finest Nora or Hamlet or Faust or Phaedra or Winnie. But beyond the already grandiose aim of giving the definitive performance of a work, a role, a score, there is a further, even higher standard which applies to dancers in a way I think does not apply to singers or actors or musicians. One can be not just the best performer of certain roles but the most complete exhibit of what it is to be a dancer.

In any performing art which is largely repertory – that is, arts in which works from the past (including the very recent past) are performed repeatedly – interest naturally flows to the contribution of the performer or executant. The work already exists. What is new, each time, is what this performer, these performers, bring to it in the way of new energies, changes in emphasis or interpretation. How they make it different, or better. Or worse. The relation of work to performer is a musical-structural one: theme and variations. A given play or opera or sonata or ballet is the theme; all the readings of it will be, to some extent, variations.

But here as well, although the dancer does what all performers or executants of a work do, dance differs from the other performing arts. For the standard against which dancers measure themselves, their performances, is not simply that of the highest excellence – as it is with actors and singers and musicians. The standard is nothing less than perfection.

In my experience, no species of performing artist is as self-critical as a dancer. I have gone backstage many times to congratulate a friend or acquaintance who is an actor or a pianist or a singer on his or her superlative performance; invariably my praise is received without much demurral, with evident pleasure (my purpose, of course, *is* to give pleasure), and sometimes with relief. But each time I've congratulated a friend or acquaintance who is a dancer on a superb performance, I've heard first a disconsolate litany of mistakes that were made: a beat was missed, a foot not pointed in the right way, there was a near slippage in some intricate partnering manoeuvre. Never mind that perhaps not only I but everyone else failed to observe these mistakes. They were made. The dancer knew. Therefore the performance was not *really* good. Not good enough.

In no other art can one find a comparable gap between what the world thinks of a star and what the star thinks about himself or herself, between the adulation that pours in from the outside and the relentless dissatisfaction that goads one from within. The degree and severity of a dancer's self-criticism is not simply a case of a performer's raw nerves (virtually all great performing artists are worriers, skilled at self-criticism), of artistic conscience – a *déformation professionelle*. It is, rather, integral to the dancer's *formation professionelle*. Part of being a dancer is this sometimes cruelly self-punishing objectivity about oneself, about one's shortcomings, as viewed from the perspective of an Ideal Observer, one more exacting than any real spectator could ever be: the god Dance.

Every serious dancer is driven by notions of perfection – perfect expressiveness, perfect technique. What this means in practice is not that anyone is perfect, but that performance standards are always being raised.

The notion of progress in the arts has few defenders now. If Balanchine was the greatest choreographer who ever lived (an unverifiable proposition firmly held by many balletomanes, myself among them), it is surely not because he came after Noverre and Petipa and Fokine, because he was the last (or the most recent) of the breed. But there does seem to be something like linear progress in the

performance of dance – unlike the other performing arts devoted largely to repertory, such as opera. (Was Callas greater than Rosa Ponselle or Claudia Muzio? The question does not make sense.) There seems no doubt that the general level of dancing in unison in companies like the Kirov and the New York City Ballet (who have probably the two best *corps de ballet* in the world) and the prowess and power and expressiveness of the leading dancers in today's great ballet companies (the two just mentioned, the Paris Opéra Ballet, the Royal Ballet, and the American Ballet Theatre – among others) are far higher than the level of the most admired dancing of the past. All dance writers agree that, a few immortal soloists apart, the dancing in Diaghilev's Ballets Russes was by today's standards technically quite limited.

As in sport or athletics, the achievement by a virtuoso dancer raises the achievable standard for everybody else. But dance demands a degree of service greater than in any other performing art, or sport. While the daily life of every dancer is a full-time struggle against fatigue, strain, natural physical limitations and those due to injuries (which are inevitable), dance itself is the enactment of an energy which must seem, in all respects, untrammelled, effortless, masterful, and at every moment fully mastered. The dancer's performance smile is not so much a smile as simply a categorical denial of what he or she is actually experiencing – for there is some discomfort, and often pain, in every major stint of performing.

It is often said that dance is the creation of illusion: for example, the illusion of a weightless body. (This might be thought of as the furthest extension of the phantasm of a body without fatigue.) But it would be more accurate to call it the staging of a transfiguration.

Dance enacts being both completely in the body and transcending the body. It is, or seems to be, finally, a higher order of attention, where physical and mental attention become the same.

Great dancers like Suzanne Farrell and Mikhail Baryshnikov project a state of total focus, total concentration, which is not simply – as for an actor or a singer or a musician – the necessary prerequisite for producing a great performance. It *is* the performance, the very centre of it.

Merce Cunningham and Lincoln Kirstein have both offered as a definition of dance: a spiritual activity in physical form. No art lends itself so aptly as dance does to metaphors borrowed from the spiritual life. (Grace. Elevation . . .) Which means, too, that all discussion of the dance and of great dancers, including this one, fit dance into some larger rhetoric about human possibility.

© *Susan Sontag, 1987. This is an abridged version of the original text.*

Bill T Jones, 1993

ANNIE LEIBOVITZ

A PERFECT OBSESSION
Interview by Clare Farrow

*A*nnie Leibovitz has gained international fame and recognition for her photographs of celebrities featured on the pages and covers of magazines, from Rolling Stone *in the 70s to* Vanity Fair *in the 80s and 90s. Less well known, perhaps, are her dance photographs. Shot mostly in black and white, in or out of the studio, Leibovitz's photographs question and experiment. Why should a dancer be shot in motion? Why photograph the entire body? Why not free the dancer from the constraints of gravity? In the following interview, conducted on 12 July 1993, Annie Leibovitz explains how these pictures came about.*

Clare Farrow: *Can you explain why you prefer to shoot dance movement in black and white rather than in colour? And, given the choice, do you like to photograph dancers in the nude?*

Annie Leibovitz: I think dance looks beautiful in black and white. Colour tends to become more conceptual. Some of the early dance photographs, and the pictures that came out of the White Oak Dance Project in 1990, were really studies in natural light. I tried to use colour, but I didn't think it was successful. There are ways to simplify it, by basically having three colours: the skin, what the dancer wears (say, black), and a grey background. But I haven't yet been able to make the colour as beautiful. My starting to get more deeply involved in dance work marked my return to black and white. This doesn't mean that there can't be colour photographs of dance. I hope to take some that I like, because I'm trying to develop a more natural look in the colour in my editorial and assignment work. There is high speed colour negative film which I've been using, trying to relax the colour. Still, I know that a black and white picture will be beautiful, whereas I feel I'm always taking a chance with colour.

I did the programme for a dance benefit for AIDS this Fall, organised by a group called DIFFA (Design Industry Fashion for AIDS), in which fashion designers collaborated with dancers. I shot colour for that, but the photographs that I like are in black and white. Unfortunately, I didn't care for the clothes. This was the first time that I'd worked with Bill T Jones and I really wanted to *see* Bill T Jones. I took him up to the roof of a building and shot him without any clothes. I ended up taking the clothes off everybody! So this dance programme will have to have the clothes shot separately with paper dolls in the back, so you can cut them out and put them on the nude dancers. (Laughter)

– Do you always take the vital elements or spirit of the choreography into account when you're photographing a dancer, or do you sometimes simply respond to the body that you see?

I found it very interesting to photograph Stephen Petronio because he shaves his head. I did a front and back shot of him, and he looks lizardy and gangly. It's a very strange coupling of pictures.

Sometimes I go off the mark but the dancer will always take me back. That's what's interesting in the rehearsal picture of Mikhail Baryshnikov and Mark Morris, the one where they're both doing the same movement. It was so beautiful to watch them. One of the things I like most to do is to watch a dance class or rehearsal. For me it's better than the performance. This picture is interesting because you see two dancers doing exactly the same movement, but you see the years of classical training that Misha has behind him and you see Mark's modern dance training. Misha is following Mark, but you're seeing two completely different worlds.

When I was working on the DIFFA project I did what dancers hate most, which is that when they walk into the photographer's studio the photographer asks them to jump. It's a cliché. Every photographer thinks that a dance photograph is a jump. But I thought that if I had this group of eight or nine dancers in the air, it would look extraordinary as a lay-out. So I had to explain to them, 'Please forgive me, I'm asking you to do this terrible thing, but I think it will be interesting to try it.' It was maybe 30 per cent successful. Stephen Petronio was one of the more successful photographs. He's off the ground but contorted. He wouldn't know how to do it any other way. I was photographing Gregory Hines and Tommy Tune together and they said, 'We're sorry, but we don't ever leave the ground, we love the ground, the ground is our friend.' I tried to explain, 'I'm not really asking you to be way up in the air. Even doing a step or a half step you could be off the ground.' But there was no convincing them. They stayed on the ground. So it didn't turn out the way I thought it might. In the Stephen Petronio photograph, you can really see his style, doing a movement as only he would do it. For Bill T Jones, I put a white backdrop on the roof, and you could see the water towers. In one photo he's just standing there, and there are two or three in which he's jumping. I think he took my direction a little too literally and there's a tendency for dancers, even when they are also choreographers, to slip into something that isn't particularly them. Bill T Jones's jumps could have been anybody's. So I keep going back to the photograph where he's just standing there, looking aggressive. I

Stephen Petronio, 1993

ABOVE: Paul Taylor with Kathy McCann, Kate Johnson, Christopher Gillis and Elie Chaib, 1990; BELOW: Mark Morris, 1990

like him that way.

For the Alvin Ailey American Dance Theater poster, I worked with a group of dancers. I went to five evenings of public performance, and I came away with the feeling that I didn't want to take a specific step or movement from one of Ailey's dances, which I think can look too posed. I felt the picture should be about the whole company, about their energy and spirit. So I wanted to put a group of them together, moving in one direction, almost like an army. I didn't have to tell them how to do it. They have all those years of training that's going to tell them how to do it. I think they liked this idea. It created a wonderful atmosphere in which to take the picture. I had to look for a way to represent 35 years of their dancing together. It had to be about the sense of community within them.

After I did the group shots the artistic director, Judith Jamison, came in for her own shooting. She was a great dancer. And my picture is still a dance picture because dance is still in her. It's in her neck – she's just turning her head to the right, away from the camera – and the dance is there.

I also like the Mark Morris picture where he's in the woods, because it was a huge discovery for me that a dancer didn't have to be standing up. He could be lying down, and the dance still comes through.

– Have you done any studies that concentrate on just a part of the dancer's body?
Yes. The feet of Misha and Twyla Tharp. Misha told me he hates his feet. But I think his feet are beautiful. I found it a charming way to deal with such famous dancers.

– Do you find when you're photographing a choreographer that there's a tension about who is in control?
I haven't met one dancer or choreographer who doesn't want the photographer to direct the shoot. Misha was the first dancer I ever photographed for *Vanity Fair*, for a cover, and he was so fed up with dance photographs, he wasn't going to do any kind of dance or jump. He came into the studio and was so against dance photography that one really had to entertain him. For me to squeeze out the few photographs that look like dance was an achievement with him because he has been photographed so much that he really can't stand walking into a photographer's studio. Practically every photographer is going to ask him to leap, and as he gets older, and has had knee injuries, he can't really leap, it's not going to be the way it was when he was 25 or 35, and he doesn't want to even attempt it. The first photographs that I did of him were some body portraits and then he asked me to do the programme for the American Ballet Theater. He said to me, 'I don't want you to do any dance pictures, I just want you to do portraits.' But there was a young Russian dancer – and Russian dancers are all leapers – and I sneaked a leaping photograph. So when I started I shared that way of thinking too, that dance photography is about getting in the air, because those pictures can be so exciting. One picture I did of Misha for the

dance programme was of him sitting in a Mustang convertible. He was the director of the company, and I wanted an image of him being in control, as you are behind the wheel of a car. He was very happy with that picture. As for the work I do now, when I have dancers in the studio I assume that most of them don't want to jump. They don't want to do dance pictures, they want something new. And every so often I get a dancer with whom I can really play or experiment.

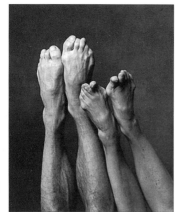

– Do you ever get dancers to improvise movements and then shoot them as they do so?
It usually doesn't last very long. The dancers do have ideas, but a dancer's life is taking directions. And this attitude comes with them into the photographer's studio. I have to have some ideas ready. I don't really want them to do exactly what I'm asking them to do, but occasionally we get stalled somewhere along the line and it's important to keep them going. And they do expect someone else to be in charge. The photograph of Paul Taylor and his dancers had to do with this. Taylor is dressed and the dancers are nude. The choreographer is in control and the dancers are vulnerable. The dancers are at the mercy of the choreographer.

– Have you experimented with long exposures, or any other techniques, to convey the blurred impression of a body in motion?
When I did the American Dance Theater shoot, I had to photograph 12 dancers and I did do a long exposure. But I didn't really like it. And then I shot Bill T Jones and I tried to do the same thing. I took him up to the roof in the evening light, which meant that automatically the image would be blurred. I've always admired Alexey Brodovitch's blurred dance photographs. In fact, when I went down to do the White Oak Dance Project I told Mark and Misha that if I had 20 pages of blurs, I would be happy. But then I got caught up in something else. It was the first time that I'd had the chance to set up a natural light studio in the middle of the woods, and I fell in love with the light and what it did to the bodies. But I did do one blurred shot. I asked them to gather in the woods, take their clothes off, and move just a little. Then I realised that they didn't have to move. I could move the camera!

– Given the choice, do you like to photograph dancers out of the studio?
I think the next time I do some dance pictures, I'm going to go out into the middle of a big field, get myself a motorcycle with a side car, let the dancers go wild, and just try to keep up with them.

The studio is beautiful though. I use either natural light or, if the light is going, I mix natural light with the strobe light. But natural light is the most beautiful, and not just for shooting dancers. And I'm trying hard to make the strobe light look natural. When I did the American Dance Theater work, I built a huge light box about 20 feet long to simulate natural light. But there's

Twyla Tharp and Mikhail Baryshnikov, 1992

White Oak Dance Project, 1990, ABOVE: Reportage Rehearsal Shot; BELOW: Underwater Dancers

White Oak Dance Project, 1990, ABOVE: Mark Morris and Mikhail Baryshnikov; BELOW: Underwater Dancers

49

David Parsons, 1991

something about the dancer always having to return to a spot on the set, or having to stay within a definite area, that's very limiting. I prefer being outdoors. There's no problem with the ceiling height, no problem with having to come back to a mark on the floor.

Going back to your question about improvisation, there was a shoot where I was trying to get David Parsons into the air. But he had stopped listening to me and had dropped to the floor and started to crawl across the floor, and I shot him doing this. To me, it's one of the strongest dance photographs I've taken. And I never would have dreamed of shooting a dancer crawling across the floor.

– Do you find modern experimental dancers more interesting to photograph than those who have been classically trained?
No. They're both interesting. They're both beautiful to me. When you see a classical dancer move, you see someone who comes from a very special place. Misha is still beautiful in that way. I admire his modern dance work, but you always see that he was trained as a classical dancer. No, I don't have a preference. I love to see a dancer just sitting in a chair, because they sit in a different way than you or I do. Even when you see them outside their classes and they're just standing there, leaning against the wall, they're still beautiful. I admire so much the ability to express oneself with the body.

There's a picture of Twyla which is interesting because you can see what she is like just from her head, her nervousness and her energy. I think a dance picture could be just the head.

– Can you talk a little more about your dance reportage work?
I photographed the American Ballet Theater when Misha was the director. But the White Oak Dance Project in 1990 was the first time I'd spent so much time on one subject since I went on tour with the Rolling Stones in 1976. I spent three or four weeks at White Oak in Florida, attending the rehearsals every day. I loved not being able to think about anything else. The ideas really started to flow. Of course, I'm trained to become obsessed. That's the nature of my work. But after the experience of the Rolling Stones tour, I became very careful about what subjects I want to spend a lot of time with. The White Oak Dance Project was an entirely different experience. It was the ideal subject to get obsessed with.

– Is it possible to draw any parallels between dance and photography?
Maybe in terms of the balance and the sense of that perfect moment when everything is in the right place, the moment when it works. In the David Parsons photograph, where he's crawling across the floor, part of his foot is chopped off on the left-hand side of the picture, and this makes it look like it really is just caught. And that's what did happen. Afterwards, we did it over and over again, but these were pictures which showed the complete body, and they didn't work. In that

particular photograph, perfection is non-perfection. Off-balance can be balance.

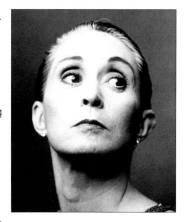

– Have you looked at the work of other dance photographers?
Of course. My idea when I went to watch the White Oak Dance Project rehearsals, was that I was going to follow one dance all the way through – the dance that Mark Morris was making. I was thinking of Barbara Morgan's book on Martha Graham. The way they worked was that Martha would finish a dance, Barbara would see it, she would go away and think about it, and then she would call up Martha in the middle of the night and say, 'I'm ready to take the picture!' It was such an important book. Paul Taylor has said it was these pictures that made him want to become a dancer.

– Is dance photography something that you might do for yourself, as a way of experimenting, outside your commissions and magazine assignments?
It's something that I started off doing for myself. But now every time a dance shoot comes up at *Vanity Fair*, they assign it to me because they know that I'm interested in dance. Every time I take a picture I have the freedom to experiment. A lot of the time what happens is dictated by how much time I have, how much time the dancer has, what the weather is like. I had to go through a period of working with the formality of the studio, and I still shoot there. But I like to get out of the studio. I prefer not to be a slave to where the light is. And the bigger the space the better. I shot the Alvin Ailey Dance Group on a beautiful rocky beach, but a dancer needs a solid floor and there was not much there that they could dance on. (Laughter) I remember some shots I took of an Olympic swimmer. I wanted to photograph her in a lake, but she'd never been out of a swimming pool. And it scared her. She couldn't see the bottom.

– Do you like to work with just one dancer, or do you like the interaction between a number of dancers?
I like to work with one or two. That's why I admire Barbara Morgan, because she could photograph large groups. It's choreography. You've got to know exactly what you want to do. We were talking before about improvising shots. When I was working on the White Oak Dance Project, I did one session with the dancers in the swimming pool. There were about eight or nine dancers in the water, and I put half on one side of the pool, half on the other side, and said to them, 'Okay now go!' They would just swim past each other and then come back and do it again. I went under the water to shoot them. I could stay under for about a minute, but I had to be held down by my assistant's foot on my back because I kept floating to the top! I liked getting the dancers off their feet. And afterwards, looking at those pictures, I realised that the dancers were actually free, free from gravity, the thing they fight their whole lives. It was quite beautiful to see what they could do without those constraints.

Twyla Tharp, 1989

51

Void, *1989, fibreglass and pigment, 121.9 x 121.9 x 91.4 cm, photo Anthony Oliver*

ANISH KAPOOR

THEATRE OF LIGHTNESS, SPACE AND INTIMACY
by Clare Farrow

O ne sees the weight of a block of cast iron which sinks in the sand, the fluidity of water and the viscosity of syrup . . . When I say that I see a sound, I mean that I echo the vibration of the sound with my whole sensory being, and particularly with that sector of myself which is susceptible to colours . . . If a phenomenon – for example, a reflection or a light gust of wind – strikes only one of my senses, it is a mere phantom, and it will come near to real existence only if, by some chance, it becomes capable of speaking to my other senses. Maurice Merleau-Ponty [1]
Il faut être léger comme l'oiseau, et non comme la plume. Paul Valéry [2]

Merleau-Ponty's words, from his writings on sense experience in *Phenomenology of Perception*, strike a note of sudden clarity when considered in parallel with the deep blue powders, the contained intimate spaces and the seemingly endless voids of suspended colour and time in the work of Anish Kapoor. Ponty describes the body as being 'a ready-made system of equivalents and transpositions from one sense to another. The senses translate each other,' he writes, 'without any need of an interpreter, and are mutually comprehensible without the intervention of any idea.'[3] To comprehend Ponty's words, or rather to experience their meaning, one has only to stand directly in front of Kapoor's *Void*, a hemisphere of fibreglass enveloped in dark Prussian-blue powdered pigment, and, most importantly of all, to dismiss all thoughts from one's mind. Don't start by thinking, this is blue so this must refer to the sky, to the depths of the sea, to the conditions of fluidity and lightness . . . Don't start by remembering the texts you have read about Kapoor. These things are valid, important even. But you can think about them later. To begin with, just give yourself to the experience of looking.

Because of the shape and texture of *Void*, the colour seems to float, rather like the colours in a Rothko painting, hovering in the space and darkening towards the centre. There is no point of focus and the colour is so pure, so concentrated, that the experience is like looking into bright sunlight – the colour is felt as an intense vibration in the eye that momentarily blinds and saturates the consciousness, inducing a feeling of vertigo. Kapoor says, 'I have always felt drawn towards some notion of fear in a very visual sense, towards sensations of falling, of being pulled inwards, of losing one's sense of self.'[4] The feeling is one of being drawn into a mysterious, somehow magical space, of being overwhelmed by pure primary colour, just as Ponty describes the experience of looking up into a very blue sky: 'I do not possess it in thought . . . I abandon myself to it and plunge into this mystery . . . it "thinks itself within me" . . . my consciousness is saturated with this limitless blue.'[5] The blue powder itself, though static, seems to have a potential for lightness and mobility, in the sense that a light wind might transform the powder into a vaporous cloud of coloured dust; and this potential for transformation on the part of the material adds to the feeling of 'sensual uncertainty' – a term that Kapoor uses when talking about his work. The sensations of dizziness and uncertainty, of being irresistibly drawn into the unknown, bring about an almost uncontrollable desire to touch, which the artist himself explains:

Over a number of years I have been working towards a sense of intimacy which has come about through a certain fragility and sensual uncertainty. It has to do with recognising that sculpture is not of the mind or not just of the mind. In order to work, at first and perhaps even in the end, it must acknowledge and remain with the body. Intimacy is much more about two hands touching than about two voices speaking. Every time I do a show people seem to be drawn to touching the works. One of the things I am clearly working with is how the hand and the eye somehow need to reaffirm each other. There is a degree of uncertainty confronting the eye which can only be resolved by extending the hand.

This sense of intimacy and uncertainty is very present in Kapoor's recent untitled block of plaster, saturated with a deep blue powdered pigment that seems almost intoxicated as it drinks in the light. Because of the way the light performs, the eye perceives a curve of darker blue inside one end of the block – an inner space or sanctum that both invites and eludes touch. To Kapoor such actual spaces are 'somehow imaginatively contained within our own sense of self . . . like some kind of vision inside the self, of a particular resonance, a particular note.' Though the work is silent, for some reason, perhaps because of the vibrant colour, perhaps because of the curve of darker blue inside, one thinks of sound, or the passage of sound.

Once again, in *Eyes Turned Inward* – two red hemispheres seemingly suspended in the air, facing

ABOVE: Eyes Turned Inward, *1993, fibreglass and pigment, two parts, 155 x 155 x 135.5 cm;* Bright Mountain, *1993, fibreboard and paint, 140 x 231 x 147 cm, photo Stephen White; BELOW:* Untitled, *1993, limestone and pigment, 53 x 89 x 70 cm, photo Stephen White; OPPO-SITE:* Untitled, *1993, plaster and pigment, 189.5 x 76.5 x 166 cm, photo Stephen White; OVERLEAF:* Echo, *1993, five musical boxes, edition of 30, wood, patinated bronze, ceramic, acrylic, gouache and musical mechanisms*

one another, observing and listening – the senses come together. As in the blue *Void*, the red colour seems to float in the contained and yet perceptually unlimited space, darkening towards the centre; but the feelings that one experiences are strikingly different. The red is paint rather than powder, applied to a textured surface, which responds to the light in such a way as to give a more spongy quality to the colour. Looking directly into one of the hemispheres, one does not experience the same feelings of vertigo and absorption, of being drawn or pulled into a void. The red is more outgoing than the blue-black powder and more sensual too. It has a different resonance. In addition to this, the shape and positioning of the two hemispheres somehow lends both a cosmic air to the work and a consciousness of the inner self, as well as muffling ambient sound, which is something that interests the artist.

Kapoor recognises the different feelings and sensations that arise on perceiving the primary colours, especially when they have been condensed into pure, concentrated matter; and also the parallels that are sometimes drawn, particularly in reference to his own work, between the processes of art and alchemy. 'If art is about anything,' he says, 'then it must be about transformation.' The artist continues:

> Colour is a real transformer. It changes things very directly. A lot of the work I have made over the last ten years or so has been concerned with the emotional and perceptual differences that exist between a blue and a red surface. The difference is enormous . . . The surface has to do with how the light reacts, how the colour reacts, how matt the colour will be . . . Recently I've tended to work more with space, with conditioning the space in such a way as to bring about different states of being. I see different works in terms of different states of being.

In the round untitled stone, punctured rather like a fruit by a dark hole and smoothed as though by water, the void has a mysterious quality, giving the stone the air of some kind of magical container or vessel. At the same time it looks like a pebble that has been tossed by the sea and washed up on the sand. In fact the stone has been worked by the artist – 'There is a fine line between polishing and removing the marks of manufacture,' he says – and the hole contains a deep blue-black powder which absorbs the light and draws the eye and the hand into its unfathomable space. Kapoor sees the void both in terms of sound and time:

> The void is not silent. I've always thought of it as a potential space. I'm coming to think of it more and more as a transitional space, an in-between space. It's very much to do with time. I've always been interested in the idea that as an artist one can somehow look again for that very first moment of creativity, when everything is possible and nothing has actually happened. It's a space of becoming.

Part of the magic of this piece lies in its actual and imaginary presence in space. There is a certainty about the round solid stone, as definite as a full stop, and yet at the same time a fragility in the apparition of the blue-black void. Moreover, the feeling of intimacy which in much of Kapoor's art comes from looking into an exterior, contained space that can be viewed only from the front, is brought about in this piece by the round presence of the stone, by its size, and by the smallness of the space containing the powder, which is rather like an ink well.

It is perhaps not surprising, given his interest in the interaction of the senses, that Kapoor has recently begun to collaborate with dancers and musicians. He talks about the mechanical music boxes which he has made with composer Brian Elias over a period of four years with an enthusiasm that seems somehow to have taken him by surprise. Though reluctant at first to take the notion of musical boxes altogether seriously, his interest grew as he began to work through all kinds of objects and started to realise that there was in fact a way of doing it. 'I was interested,' he explains, 'in marrying the two forms, sculpture and music, in such a way that the arts are not simply imposed on one another. So I arrived at a scale, the objects being roughly nine or ten inches high and 12 inches wide. There are five of them. The central one is a bell which rings mechanically every nine seconds, like a temple bell. You wind it with a key. The other four objects are quiet and meditative. The scale is interesting because, although they're very small objects, together the sound-object conjunction occupies a vast space. This surprised me when I first discovered it . . .' After some thought he continues, 'In the end, occupying space is really an act of the imagination and a work must be able to pull in the imagination of the viewer.'

One of the main problems for any artist in doing a collaboration is the loss of total control that inevitably occurs, and this loss is something that Kapoor feels keenly. The difficulties are intensified when the artist is working with someone whose discipline is governed by very different laws and working processes. For this reason it is perhaps more straightforward for a sculptor to work with an architect than with a choreographer. Nevertheless Kapoor jumped at the chance of working with Laurie Booth when the experimental dancer and choreographer approached him to design the set for *River Run*, a performance which takes its title from the opening of James Joyce's *Finnegans Wake*. 'We were going to attempt to do a real collaboration,' Kapoor explains, 'not as Merce Cunningham and John Cage had done (though of course they were very successful, and were operating in a very different context), making the works independently

River Run, 1993, photos John Riddy

and then putting them together just before the performance. We felt that we should be doing something else, that we should really be working together. I don't know that we were entirely successful in doing that.'

Despite the artist's lingering doubts, *River Run* was warmly received when it was performed in the Queen Elizabeth Hall in London on 27 and 28 March 1993. Imagined by Booth to be a kind of journey, the interplay between the dance and the five pure white mountains of the set, which were moved around the stage during the performance, was described by critics as being fluid, silken, calm, floating, quiet and mystical. As Kapoor recalls,

Moving the mountains around the stage was a way of changing the space in which the dancers were working. It also had to do with the idea of shifting the scale from the actual to the imaginary. I think Laurie found this to be full of potential as far as the choreography was concerned.

In addition to the white mountains, at times perceived as drifting icebergs, Kapoor devised a deep red slash in the back wall, enhanced by the lighting of Michael Hulls with whom he worked quite closely, and described by the choreographer as being like 'an opening onto another dimension.' And in parallel to the improvised movement and the set was the electronic music composed by Hans Peter Kühn, a collage of sounds including creaking noises, telephones ringing, dogs barking and the composer muttering lines from *Finnegans Wake.*

'One of the exciting things about a theatrical production,' Kapoor reflects, 'is that reality is suspended. There is no here and now. It's very different to sculpture . . .' And did the experience of collaboration have any lasting influence on his work? In response to this question, the artist looked thoughtfully around his studio – a large space full of light and silence, containing among other works two unfinished mountains made out of many layers of wood that reflect the light, producing a kind of shimmer. 'Well, I'm still working with the forms of the mountains. So in that sense, yes.'

Notes

1 Maurice Merleau-Ponty, *Phenomenology of Perception*, Routledge, London, 1962, pp230, 234 and 318.
2 Paul Valéry, in Italo Calvino, 'Lightness', *Six Memos for the Next Millennium*, Jonathan Cape, London, 1992, p163.
3 Merleau Ponty, *ibid*, p235.
4 Anish Kapoor talking to Clare Farrow, 2 July 1993. All statements by the artist have been taken from this interview, conducted in the artist's studio.
5 Merleau Ponty, *ibid*, p214.

Bright Mountain, *1993, fibreboard and paint, 140 x 231 x 147 cm, photo Stephen White*

LAURIE BOOTH

THE MAKING OF RIVER RUN

*L*aurie Booth's collaborations have brought him into close working contact with a number of leading artists. In the following interview, conducted on 17 July 1993, the dancer and choreographer talks about his experience of working with Anish Kapoor on River Run.

Clare Farrow: *How did the project come about?*
Laurie Booth: I was looking into collaborations with visual artists. As a dancer my approach has been very reductionist, in the sense that I've been working on just the body itself moving in space, without having the stabilisation of a narrative, or any particular set or specific construct. The compositional work that I do deals a lot with the improvisational habit, that is, the work is continuously changed by the existential fact that there is a space with an audience. So I was looking into compositional strategies that enable and extend the basic aesthetic notion of the body and the self in space.

A few years ago I started to consider light in depth, as an environmental factor, and I became very interested in the way in which light not only defines an object, but actually creates a sense of density and directionality in the space. I found that the basic issues of dance are space, time and the kinetic experience of the body in movement. Without the experience of the body, space and time have no particular meaning. I was interested in working with visual artists who are dealing with space and also time, because visual artists do relate with time. I was very curious to know how artists handled the concept of space. Working with various people I was drawn further into this visual art way of thinking and I found that there's a useful point of contact. This also extends the modern dance tradition of collaboration between artists from different mediums. That's an important issue because it's something that has been rather lost in this country. I can't think of many choreographers who work with leading artists as opposed to set designers.

I had seen an exhibition of Anish Kapoor's paintings and drawings in the Tate and found them fascinating because they seem to be about the interior landscape of the body. They're very close to images which as a dancer you have of your body when you are in a state of deep thought about a movement. Your inner eye in a sense opens up and looks into what's going on inside. I spoke to Anish and he said that he wanted to work with a choreographer. We spent more than a year building up the

relationship before we actually got to the performance. We explored many different ways of doing it.

The words *River Run* are taken from the opening of James Joyce's *Finnegans Wake* which is *the* great book of the unconscious mind. If *Ulysses* is the book of the conscious mind, the conscious exploration of form and structure, then *Finnegans Wake* is the model of free association. Being an improviser, I wanted to touch base with that tradition. Also Hans Peter Kühn, the composer, wanted to do some work with text. But the main thing was to establish this connection between different artists.

– Have you have been influenced by the work of Merce Cunningham?
I wouldn't say that I have been directly influenced by him, but the way Merce has worked with people in the past has obviously affected us all. He has really opened up a series of possibilities and choices, for other people as well as for his own group. He has extended the range of working collaborations that can exist. He's one of the few choreographers I really admire, someone who is continuously doing something brave and interesting. My own training was very much working around compositional ideas by Cage and working with Steve Paxton who worked with Merce, so I was in that milieu when I was a student. I was very caught up with the whole thing.

– Cunningham, Cage and Rauschenberg worked independently, bringing together the dance, music and art only days before the performance.
Yes. Anish and I worked much more closely than that. I *have* worked in that way but Anish wanted to make a much more conscious set of connections and to have the dialogue working throughout the whole collaboration. That was fine by me. Artists have different ways of working, and if someone needs to work in the studio on their own, or if they don't really want to have any contact for a period of time, then I'm happy to let them get on with it. If you're working with people, an element of faith has to enter into the relationship. You have to trust that people know what they're doing. It was my project. I was directing it. But having said that, I try to give people maximum freedom.

It would be more accurate to say that the experience of elements coming together at the last moment was more true of the performance and the sound. We only got the sound track about three days before the first performance. It affected the last section quite radically. But I've worked with Hans Peter so many times now that we understand each other very well, so it wasn't such a problem.

– How did the ideas for the set develop?
Well that was interesting because originally we wanted to have a river! We tried out many different things on paper and in conversation. We would go away and think about it, and then we would come back and something would have changed. When we started getting serious about staging it we suddenly began saying, 'Look, it's not possible to do this, or if we do want to do this we've got to do it in another way, and does that then affect the original idea, and do we still want to do it this way?', and so on.

– Did you work out the dance on paper at this stage?
Only in terms of the overall shape and sense of structure, the pacing of the piece, and how it might develop. The idea for the mountains came up when we couldn't have a river and we could no longer have something hanging overhead which we had been looking at too, and various other ideas had come and gone, and then this mountain idea started to develop, until we had something like the whole of the Himalayas on stage! I think this was interesting for Anish because his work is often so abstract and to begin with the ideas were too. Then things became more and more specific, more and more real. Suddenly we were having reproductions of actual mountains on stage!

– When did you decide to move the mountains?
After the first preview performance. My idea was that they should move but somehow they had been made so that they couldn't move. But I needed them to move otherwise everything became too static. We needed to keep the idea of the fluid river running through the environment.

– There's something very magical about seeing a mountain move.
Yes, just as there is something magical about seeing a mountain from different angles, about turning a mountain around, and transforming it by changing its size, by reducing its scale.

– Did the improvised movement respond to the set?
The improvisation was set independently, so it was not open to being influenced. But on a simple level, we knew that the mountains were going to be a great source of light, because they were so white and had so many reflective surfaces. We knew this would influence the look of the movement. The costumes were also made to absorb and reflect the light. So the elements were made independently, but with the staging connections in mind. The same was true of the lighting which was designed to enhance the other elements. We knew it would work.

– How did the idea for the red slash come about?
Originally we were going to have a big red bed on stage with a gash down the middle of it. Then the bed disappeared and the gash somehow remained, though we weren't quite sure how to use it. Then we wanted to have a gash hanging front-stage but there was nowhere to hang it from and it became too difficult. Then we came up with the final technical solution of a black box against a black wall with a red light inside the box and just a gash inside. It was a very simple solution in the end. Also, quite unintentionally, we arrived at a male-female dialectic, with the phallic mountain and the red gash. That shift in the environment was very interesting.

The set establishes a field within which the compositional process can occur, where the dancers can work and rework and play with the material. The composition is continuously being brought into question by the shifting environment. Of course, there are only so many places those mountains can be, so there is a final boundary around what the audience sees and what the dancers experience, which makes it *that* piece rather than another piece.

– Do you approach improvisation in a spirit of play?
In myself, yes I do, and when we're performing I hope there's an alert and spontaneous working with the elements. The material which we use to improvise is very set. So the process is one of recombining and redefining known material.

– Do you use chance operations?
Only in the sense that the material is reassembled in different ways. The position of the mountains changes so that, say, the 19th minute looks completely different in every performance. You are seeing the same elements but the way in which they are coming together is determined by what happened in the 17th and 18th minutes.

Chance procedure means that you have chosen a certain process for selecting material. In my work, you set up certain conditions and then you just go! So the first moment of the piece to a certain extent determines the twentieth minute and the fiftieth minute, and so on. There is a kind of continuity and logical progression but I would say that it is a random procedure rather than a chance procedure.

– How do you approach time in a performance?
The time structures are determined by the sound score. I tend to let the composer know whether I want the piece to be in ten sections, or five sections, or three sections, or whether there should be clearly defined boundaries between the sections. You can define certain sections for the performers in such a way that the audience is not able to discern the sectionality of the piece. So there are those kinds of things going on.

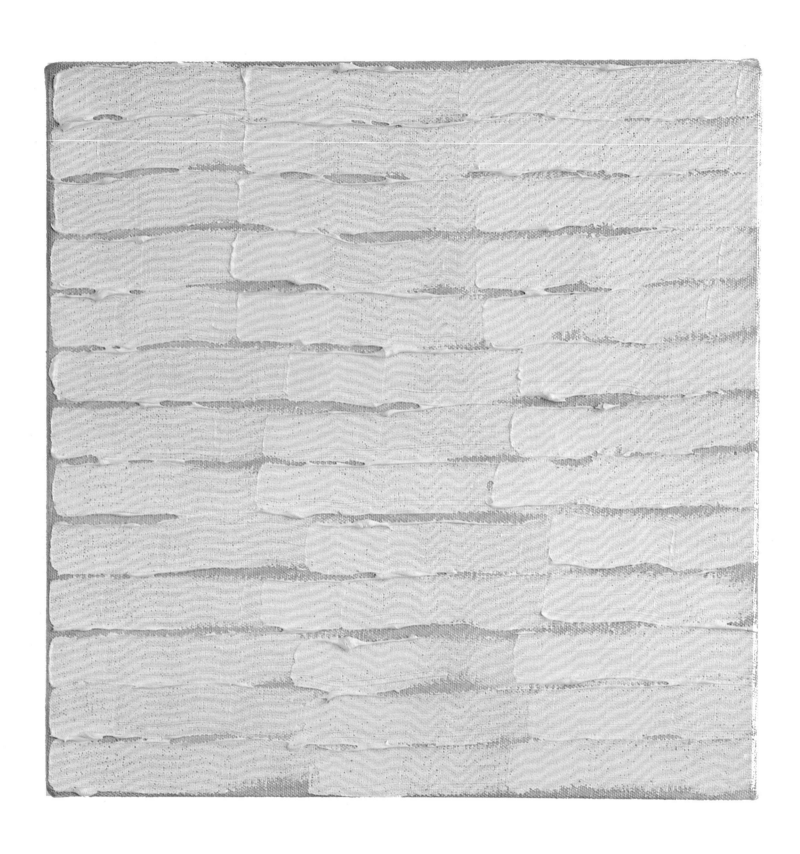

Untitled, *1965, oil on canvas, 26 x 26 cm, Lisson Gallery, London*

ROBERT RYMAN
A SEQUENCE OF VARIATIONS
by Clare Farrow

*A*n avalanche of colour has no force. Colour attains its full expression only when it is organised, when it corresponds to the emotional intensity of the artist . . . when one composes with it, like a musician with harmonies, it is simply a question of emphasising the differences.
Henri Matisse [1]

It's like listening to music . . . and feeling somehow fulfilled – that what you experienced was somehow extraordinary. It sustained you for a while. You can't explain it to someone who did not experience it. You can say they played this and they did that, but it won't make any sense at all. That's not what it is about. It was about this experience of delight and fulfillment. Robert Ryman [2]

In 1952, Robert Ryman arrived in New York with the intention of becoming a jazz musician. He played the saxophone. He found digs with other musicians near the loading dock of Bloomingdale's department store, took a number of temporary jobs, and began to study with a working jazz pianist. His surprisingly casual, inquisitive, almost playful initiation into the practice of painting has been described by the artist in his conversations with Robert Storr:

> I went in [to a nearby art-supply store] and bought some oil paint and canvas board and some brushes – they didn't have acrylic at that time – and some turpentine. I was just seeing how the paint worked, and how the brushes worked. I was just using the paint, putting it on a canvas board, putting it on thinly with turpentine, and thicker to see what that was like, and trying to make something happen without any specific idea of what I was painting.[3]

Ryman's approach seems to have been that of a tireless experimenter, filled with curiosity and free from weighty intentions, playing with the paints, brushes and surfaces, trying out different combinations and effects, as a scientist might do in his laboratory; or a photographer in his darkroom; or as a musician might do when, playing around with a few notes on a piano, he sees how many different sounds and variations can be achieved. This experimental approach, which is serious in its playfulness, has continued to be the force behind Ryman's painting. It is an approach that seems to involve a freedom that is *supported* rather than limited by a degree of control: 'I let the paint develop itself, . . .' the artist has said, 'It is a controlled

approach without controlling it . . . I simply try to let it happen.' [4] It is not surprising then to turn to Ryman's reflections on jazz, which he was to give up in 1954, having decided to turn his attentions exclusively to the practice of painting: 'I was never interested in free jazz,' he has said, again in conversation with Robert Storr, 'I was interested in jazz with a structure. It definitely had to have structure.' [5]

In 1953, Ryman became a guard at The Museum of Modern Art in New York, a position that gave him the chance to study, at length and in a visual depth unbridled by written analysis, the work of Cézanne, Matisse and Mark Rothko, among many others. In the paintings of Cézanne he noted the structure and composition – 'you wouldn't know how he did it'; in Rothko, the colour, surface, structure and 'the nakedness of it'; and in Matisse, the 'very straightforward and clear way' in which the painter worked with his materials to produce a calm serenity and visual simplicity that is *felt* purely and directly by the senses.[6] It is interesting, in fact, to consider a number of statements by Matisse, on colour and tonal harmony, in parallel to those of Ryman, whose comments are open, simple and direct, and draw attention to the limited power of words to fully express the feelings and sensations brought about by the exquisitely subtle variations of tone and surface in his paintings. To Ryman, the act of painting has nothing to do with intellectual analysis. 'You can think before you paint, you can think after you have painted, but while you are painting, thinking is the worst thing you can do,' he has said. 'The artist just does it . . . I think that it cannot be told, it cannot be written in a formula, as in A+B = good painting.' He continues: 'I have to repeat that as with all painting you need the direct experience. It is a sense of wonder and well-being that is projected by the art, whether music or painting or poetry. It is not analytically describable.' [7]

In his *Notes of a Painter*, 1908, Matisse speaks of his desire for harmony, like 'that of a musical composition', for balance, purity, lightness, serenity and 'the condensation of sensations'. He writes: 'If upon a white canvas I set down some sensations of blue, of green, of red, each new stroke diminishes the importance of the preceding ones . . . It is necessary that the various marks I use be balanced so that they do not destroy each other.' He talks about the seduction of tone, about how his choice of colours is based on 'felt experiences' and how 'a moment

OVERLEAF LEFT: Surface Veil, *1970, oil on fibreglass with waxed paper frame and masking tape, 33 x 33 cm, photo Bill Jacobson, The Museum of Modern Art, New York, Gift of the Denise and Andrew Saul Fund and the Scaler Foundation. One of 18 related paintings of the same title made between 1970 and 1972. The larger works were painted on linen or cotton canvas, the smaller ones on thin fibreglass called 'Surface Veil'; RIGHT:* Versions XII, 1991, *oil on fibreglass with wax paper, 47.6 x 43.2 cm, photo Jean-Pierre Kuhn, The Pace Gallery, New York. One of 16 paintings of the same title made between the summer of 1991 and spring 1992.*

comes when all the parts have found their definite relationships, and from then on it would be impossible for me to add a stroke to my picture without having to repaint it entirely.'[8]

Many critics have written about Ryman as a maker of 'white paintings'. In response Ryman has said, 'I don't think of myself as making white paintings. I make paintings; I am a painter. White paint is my medium.'[9] He has also stated, '[White] doesn't interfere. It's a neutral colour that allows for a clarification of nuances in painting. It makes other aspects of painting visible that would not be so clear with the use of other colours.'[10]

To say that the white of linen is the same as the white of cotton, or that the white of handmade *Lugano* paper is identical to the white of handmade *Classico* paper, or that white paint on wax paper is the same as white paint on fibreglass, or indeed that the grey of steel as a surface is not vastly different to the brown of corrugated cardboard, would be as foolish, one might argue, as to say that a note sounds the same whether it is played on a piano, a violin, a cello, a viola, an oboe, or a clarinet. In the light of Matisse's statement above, it is perhaps also interesting to consider Ryman's untitled paintings of 1962, in which the artist has applied short rhythmic strokes of thick white paint all over the canvas, and over other colours, including reds, greens and blues which bounce out at intervals. There is a feeling of movement in these paintings and a chromatic vibrancy beneath the jazzy strokes of white.

The majority of Ryman's paintings are square, a format which the artist describes as being 'neutral' and 'composed'. Occasionally a rectangle might appear, but only as an exception that proves the rule. The white applied to a surface is the other constant in Ryman's work. This much stays the same. But the white could be oil, by itself or combined with blue chalk or gesso for example; it could be acrylic, enamel or pastel; it could be a warm or a cold white, matt or varnished; it could be any white or combination of whites. As for the surface, it could be fibreglass with a waxed paper frame; linen or cotton canvas, stretched or unstretched; it could be aluminium with steel bolts; Bristol board or Gator

board; fibreglass panel with aluminium; plastic or steel; it could be any one or combination of surfaces, light or heavy, hard or soft, fragile and thin perhaps, like the waxed paper, smooth or textured with a particularly sensual weave. As Ryman says:

The surface . . . has its own presence and its own structure which can have a certain beautyı . . . The process does not begin with the application of paint on a surface, rather with the material of the surface and the construction of the surface itself. When the application of paint begins, it is not just a matter of what the paint does in and of itself, but also, how the paint will change the surface into 'something to see'.[11]

The way in which the white is applied also comes into play: the size of the brush, the length of the stroke, the loading of the brush, how it is pulled across the surface, whether in one long stroke (like a note sustained on one breath) or in short rhythmic staccato movements; the direction in which the paint is pulled, how sensitive it is to the light, whether masking tape has been used in the process, leaving traces in the composition, whether the paint is applied softly or not, whether the edges of the frayed cotton or raw linen are left bare or not. Then there is the way in which the painting is attached to the wall: it could be taped, for example, or bolted, or stapled, or fastened, or nailed . . . The variations are endless. The tonal richness astounding. But only if you spend time with the painting and allow yourself to be moved by it. As Ryman says:

There are other ways of seeing, other possibilities . . . Painters – well, their perception and their vision may be a little more highly tuned, you might say . . . Experiencing painting is a matter of letting yourself be open to the painting, or to the music. You need to be open and let the painting come to you, which is a very difficult thing to explain . . . If you approach a painting from a preconceived analytical position, you are not going to understand it and you are not going to experience it, because you are trying to force something. You have to just let it happen, to let the painting itself speak. If you can do that, then you can have the experience.[12]

Notes

1 Matisse, 'The Role and Modalities of Colour', 1945; see Jack D Flam (ed), *Matisse on Art*, Phaidon Press, Oxford, 1978, p99.
2 Ryman talking to Robert Storr, Oct 1986; see Storr's text on the artist, 'Simple Gifts', *Robert Ryman,* Tate Gallery, London and The Museum of Modern Art, New York, 1993, pp9-45.
3 Ryman to Robert Storr, June 1992, *ibid*, p12.
4 Ryman to Urs Raussmüller, 'A Talk in Ryman's Studio', New York, April 1992, in *Robert Ryman: Versions,* catalogue published to coincide with exhibitions at the Hallen für neue Kunst, Schaffhausen, May-Oct 1992

and The Pace Gallery, New York, Dec 1992-Jan 1993.
5 Ryman to Robert Storr, 1992.
6 See Robert Storr, 'Simple Gifts', pp12-13.
7 Ryman to Urs Raussmüller, 1992.
8 Matisse, 'Notes of a Painter', 1908; see Jack D Flam (ed), *Matisse on Art*, pp 37 and 38.
9 Phyllis Tuchman, 'An Interview with Robert Ryman', *Artforum*, May 1971, p46.
10 Ryman in Nancy Grimes, 'White Magic', *Art News*, Summer 1986, p89.
11 Ryman to Urs Raussmüller, 1992.
12 *Ibid*.

OPPOSITE: Versions XVI, 1991-92, oil on fibreglass, 36.2 x 33 cm, photo Ellen Page Wilson, The Pace Gallery, New York

Mott Willis and grandson, Crystal Springs, Mississippi, 1973

VAL WILMER
SHOOTING THE BLUES

*T*urn to any book on the history of jazz and
you are bound to come across the photographs of Val Wilmer. There may be
*pictures by other photographers, showing the heat,
smoke and shining instruments of performances by
Charlie Parker, say, or Dizzy Gillespie. But, almost
certainly, it will be the images recorded by Wilmer, in
Harlem, or Chicago or New Orleans, that will linger
on in your mind as you turn the pages and finally put
the book back on the shelf. 'The musicians are about
more than just playing the instruments,' Wilmer says
in the following interview by Clare Farrow, and much
of the power of her photography, which has always
been partnered by her writing, lies in the fact that as
a photo-journalist she has delved deep into her
subject, developing a profound respect both for the
individual musicians and for the innovations and
origins of the music. Whether documenting the still
moments in-between the playing, or the vibrancy of
a parade in New Orleans, or the spirit of the blues on
a porch in Mississippi, there is a conviction in
Wilmer's photography that never wavers, a belief
that the power of African-American music lies in its
celebration of life, in spite of everything.*

Clare Farrow: *You were 15 when you first photographed Louis Armstrong, using a box Brownie
camera. Did this mark the beginning of your interests in jazz and photography?*
Val Wilmer: I was a jazz fan from the age of 11 or 12.
There was a long period when American artists
didn't play freely in this country because of union
restrictions. These were lifted in 1956. It was quite
an amazing occasion when Louis Armstrong came. I
was a bit too young to recognise exactly what was
happening but the coverage in the newspapers was
extraordinary. I went to see him play in the Empress
Hall in Earls Court. Louis was quite a writer you know
– he used to write on a typewriter with two fingers –
and while he was there the *Daily Express* serialised
his diary over four days. All the local musicians had
come to see him off. Suddenly there he was and I
took his picture.
   I sort of fell into jazz through a combination of
circumstances. I wasn't unaware of rock 'n roll of
course. My friends were listening to Elvis and Bill
Haley and Little Richard and I was too. But jazz
seemed more substantial. It has more depth. Some
people who study jazz can spend weeks on end
trying to find out who played the two bars on clarinet
at the end of a particular track recorded 50 years

ago. I was just lucky that I met some of those people
early on, writers and collectors who were involved in
those things.

*– The photo-journalist is a traveller, an observer, a
documenter, a researcher, to a degree detached
and 'invisible'. Do you see yourself in these terms?*
A lot of photographers have deluded themselves into
thinking that they are detached. Nobody is really
detached. Even the most straightforward news
photographers are not detached. They are putting
forward their own versions of events. There was a
time when I wanted to be detached but I don't think I
was very good at it. I was always involved with the
music and with the musicians.
   It's not by chance that we talk about 'shooting'
pictures and 'taking' pictures. The camera is a kind
of licence. It is also something to hide behind. After
all if it wasn't for the camera, how would I or any other
photographer have entered worlds other than our
own? If you have a camera you can just come off the
street and knock on somebody's door. You feel that
you've got a right somehow, and this creates
situations that are often abused.

*– Did you encounter many problems as a woman
photographer in the world of black music?*
The main problems that I experienced as a woman
photographer came from the people around the
musicians, the stage managers for instance. There
was a kind of smutty attitude around which was
difficult. I didn't know any other women taking
photographs in the music world then. The musicians
were different though. They were artists, they had
seen it all, they had been on the road, they knew the
score.

*– You have said that you 'try to let the musicians
speak direct.' Do you believe that the photographs
can speak for themselves?*
I thinks words are often necessary. I like my photographs to appear with some text and sometimes it's
my own text. I am a writer as well as a photographer.
The idea of putting the musician's point across, and
sometimes using the musician's own words to
accompany the photograph, really comes from
being an interviewer myself.

*– Many of your pictures seem to be taken in the spirit
of improvisation. There is often movement – a
blurred hand playing an instrument or beating out a*

Monk and Wade, Village Vanguard, New York, 1972

rhythm – and a feeling of spontaneity, as if the music is only just beneath the surface, at all times. You also seem to be drawn to the ordinary moments before and after the playing, whether it be Louis Armstrong in a recording session or Mott Willis sitting with a guitar between his knees on a porch in Mississippi.

Photography *is* improvisation. I'm trying to do something other than the obvious, reacting against the editors I met along the way who wanted every line on someone's face to be in focus. I don't want that. I would like to convey an idea of the music. African-American music is always slightly off the beat. To its critics that makes it appear random and out of tune. To those who understand it, it presents a different way of playing a melody, of playing a note. To give an example: Through the innovations in that music the whole concept of playing instruments in the symphony orchestra has changed. It's a very powerful music which challenges received ways of listening.

Photographs that are posed and contrived can look like advertising shots. Photography requires a lot of concentration and modern technology has made it easy to forget this. You see a lot of pictures of musicians where all the photographer has done is to point the camera and take the picture. There isn't anything technically wrong with the photograph but it doesn't have any action in it, it doesn't have any feeling. You have to watch your subjects playing and wait for them to do something different, otherwise it's a picture we've all seen a thousand times.

The reason for photographing those in-between moments is that the musicians are about more than just playing the instruments or singing – and let's not forget that the voice is an instrument too. When we're talking about black music we're talking about artists who have seldom been given the respect that they deserve. It's fine for some to be treated as icons, like Miles or Louis, but sometimes it's as if these artists aren't real. They are people who have a family behind them and a culture and I would like to show them as being a little bit more human, to go beyond the stereotypes. At the same time, by showing them as ordinary people, as people who have the same desires, cares and joys that we have ourselves, that's my way of giving them the respect that they deserve.

– Have you sought to capture the mood of the blues in your work?

White people tend to think the blues is a music of sorrow and pain. It isn't. It's a music of celebration. It says, we're here despite everything. Archie Shepp, the saxophonist, has said, 'Jazz is a symbol of the triumph of the human spirit. It is a lily in spite of the swamp.' That's what I believe. It is a belief, it's not just some kind of intellectual thought. If you ask African-American musicians what the blues means to them, most will say that it is a music of joy, of getting down and having fun, of celebration. They won't say that it's a music about the cotton fields.

Some people may say that. But most will tell you that it's about happiness.

It has been said before that music is the thread that binds black people. It is a language that was created as a means of self-affirmation and a way of telling the outside world, we're here despite the fact that we don't *appear* to have a great literature. Music is the alternative. Some people choose to see poverty in these photographs. But the majority will see the warmth and humanity – it sounds as if I'm saying this about my photographs but I'm actually saying it about the people who welcomed me into their lives. I found them through musicians and people who wrote about the music. Very few people did I meet just like that. I knew where I was going and I went there. But I didn't know what I was going to find when I went to the South, I didn't know which particular dirt road I was going to follow.

The music is vibrant and life-enhancing, for the people who play it and for their communities. In any black community music is an essential part of every kind of gathering.

– In African-American music, the instrument is seen as the counterpart of the voice. In your photograph of Dédé Pierce in New Orleans, the trumpet seems to be a part of the musician, an extension of the self.

All music is an extension of the human voice, all the true musicians have a cry or a shout in their playing. I know what you're talking about, but in terms of the photographs it's not a conscious thing.

– Your pictures taken in Mississippi, New Orleans, North and South Carolina, New York and Chicago, seem to trace the history and development of jazz, for instance the fact that blues came out of religious music. In this sense, do you see your work in terms of historical documentation?

For people of my generation it was part of the learning process to take on board all the history of the music and to know where it came from. This seems to be less important to more recent generations of those listeners who come from outside the music's community which is something that I find distressing. It may be inevitable. When I first started taking pictures I knew that I wanted to photograph the musicians. I was really more interested in writing than in photography to start off with. I was always snapping away but I didn't take myself particularly seriously. Then one morning in 1971 I woke up and thought, I'm 29 years old, I've always wanted to go to New Orleans, to hear blues in the South, to experience the churches, I can't wait until I'm older and have more money, I've just got to go. I bought a Greyhound bus ticket and made plans about who I was going to stay with and I went. That was my idea, to go to New Orleans and to listen to the blues wherever I could find it. I had been writing for

ABOVE: Jacob Stuckey, Bentonia, Mississippi, 1973; BELOW: Cousin Joe, Roosevelt Sykes and Rev 'Gatemouth' Moore, New Orleans, 1973

Rehearsing on Prince Street, *Ornette Coleman Quartet: Ornette Coleman, Ed Blackwell,*
Dewey Redman Coleman and Charlie Haden, New York, 1971

Complete Communion, *Jazzmobile audience, Harlem, New York, 1967*

Dédé Pierce, Preservation Hall, New Orleans, 1972

Melody Maker, which was then a serious music paper, since 1966, and I continued to do this, interviewing blues people in the South and a lot of the revolutionary musicians who were involved in the music that was going on in New York in the 70s.

– *In* The Face of Black Music *you have quoted BB King as saying, 'the blues was a language we invented to let people know we had something to say,' and drummer Billy Higgins, 'You can't go back with music, you got to go straight ahead. Whites haven't really exploited jazz because they can't hold on to it. As soon as they think it's here, it's there. It doesn't stand still, it's always moving.' Do you want to convey these points in your work?*
It's very important to recognise that all innovations in this music have come from African-Americans. They've all been copied, codified, exploited and in many cases abused by whites. Some white musicians are humble but many aren't. I heard a local white saxophonist interviewed on the radio recently and they said to him, 'What is jazz?', as radio interviewers do, and he didn't say anything about where it came from. I think he vaguely mentioned the names of Charlie Parker and John Coltrane. But he didn't use the word black, he didn't say African-American, and frankly I find that out of order. I'm not an advocate of separatism in any shape or form, but the fact is it's self-evident that the music is the creation of African-American people and, whether I'm writing or taking photographs, I would like to convey that point. In my recent exhibition in London [at The Special Photographers Company] which I called *Jazz Roots and Branches* I have included some pictures of white musicians whom I respect because, of course, the music has developed in many directions. However, respect is due to the people who created it and I don't think it can be underlined enough that people like Louis Armstrong and Duke Ellington and Charlie Parker are the giants, the kings of modern music. There is no praise that is high enough for them.

– *Duke Ellington defined jazz in terms of the 'freedom of expression' and drummer Ed Blackwell, talking about Ornette Coleman, said that 'he used "swing" more or less as a term for playing free, for playing my own self . . .' Many of the musicians in your pictures seem to be 'playing free' in front of the camera. I'm thinking in particular of Jacob Stuckey dancing in a room in Mississippi.*
I just wanted to convey the spirit of the music. I was there photographing the guitarist Jack Owens whose house it was and Jacob Stuckey was dancing. I was fascinated by the fact that Jacob's uncle, Henry Stuckey, had taught Skip James, one of the great blues musicians. And there *I* was, dancing with Jacob too, and feeling *connected*.

– *How did you come to photograph the Jazzmobile*

in 119th Street, Harlem? Why did you turn your attention to the audience?
When I took the photograph I had no deliberate plan. I just went up to Harlem to listen to the music and I photographed the audience. I was being a photo-journalist. But it's become my favourite photograph which is quite interesting. Harlem is a complex place. Some parts of it are broken down physically and so are some of the people who live there, but it has a great spirit and it's a place of great historical importance. The essence of my work is about communion. It's about my communion with the music and the communion that the musicians have with the audience. And when that goes, when the audience isn't there to 'play the band', then the music takes on a different meaning. And that is what often happens now and I'm sorry to see it. I don't enjoy going to listen to music of any kind unless the audience is giving something back to the artists.

– *The drummer James Black has said of New Orleans, 'There's a definite originality about the music that comes from here. The rhythm is infectious. If you listen to it long enough, your foot will start going, and if your mind is free and loose, you're liable to stand up and start dancing . . .' Was this the mood you wanted to convey in your pictures taken in New Orleans?*
When I was in New Orleans, photographing the funerals and other parades, that was certainly what I was trying to do. There's something about New Orleans which makes it the most European and at the same time the most African of American cities. It's a wonderful place. There are parades all the time and they're always accompanied by the Second Line, the people dancing. All you need is a tune on a trumpet and a rhythm on a drum and people are out on the street without any provocation whatsoever. They just dance. It's very African. You feel as though you're part of something that goes back a very long way. All the talk about America having no history is meaningless when you participate in a New Orleans funeral because that goes back through many cultures, both European and African.

Val Wilmer's photographs have appeared in magazines, books, newspapers and exhibitions around the world, including shows in Paris, New York and London, at the Victoria and Albert Museum and most recently at The Special Photographers Company. Her work is represented in a number of major photographic collections, including the V&A and the Musée d'Art Moderne in Paris. She has published a number of books, including Jazz People *(1970, now available from Da Capo Press, New York),* The Face of Black Music *(Da Capo Press, 1976) and an autobiography,* Mama Said There'd Be Days Like This *(Womens Press, London, 1989). The above interview was conducted in London on 22 June 1993.*

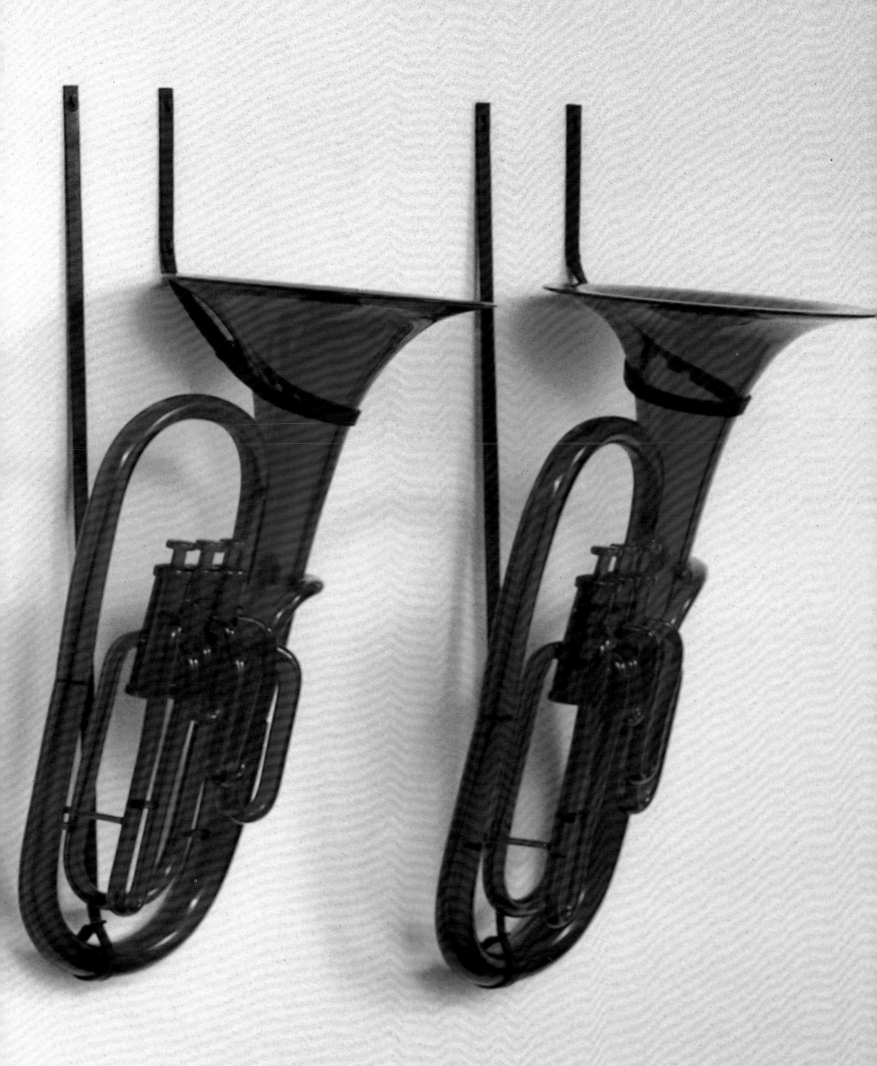

JAN VERCRUYSSE
SOUNDS OF SILENCE

T he pianos are silent. Mute and muffled. The white plaster keys produce no music. There are no strings to sound. Like children's toys, they play with the imagination. Strange assemblages of plaster, glass, iron, wood, copper. Platforms, grids and structural repetitions. Frozen. Inscrutable. Detached.

The blue glass instruments are silent too, suspended, almost restrained, by black vertical leather thongs. A trombone and two trumpets. A trombone, three trumpets and three horns. Positioned like notes on a musical stave. A visual ensemble. Contained in a curious way by horizontal sheets of glass, supported on iron. There is no music, no noise as such. But the blue Murano glass has its own particular resonance. Not the heavy shining resonance of brass. Instead it speaks of fragility and lightness. One can sense the ringing, tinkling sound that the glass would make were you to tap it lightly with a spoon. Would it be possible to slide the trombone? To press down the delicate keys of the trumpet? And what would happen were you to blow, even gently, to make a sound? The blue glass, exquisite in its fragility and translucency, would shatter. The instrument would be lost.

Tombeaux. Tombs that speak of presence and absence, music and silence, of things that seem familiar and are finally beyond comprehension. There are no answers. Only a sense of mystery and a cool disturbing beauty.   *Clare Farrow*

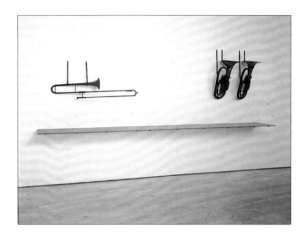

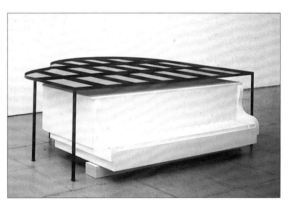

ABOVE: Tombeaux, 1991, glass, iron and leather, 196 x 375 x 30 cm, photo John Riddy; BELOW: M (M4), 1992, plaster, iron, glass and wood, 55 x 176 x 153 cm; OPPOSITE: Tombeaux, 1991, detail of above; OVERLEAF: Tombeaux, 1991, glass, iron and leather, 600 x 700 cm (overall dimensions), installation Castello di Rivoli, Turin, Collection Kunsthalle, Berne

MOMENTS IN TIME
A CENTURY OF DANCE PHOTOGRAPHY
by Judith Mackrell

Merce Cunningham once said that the reason why dance is so difficult to write about is that 'it's not so much intangible as evanescent . . . I compare . . . dance to water.' Not only is choreography too speedy and too protean an art form to pin down on paper but words themselves are frustratingly inaccurate. Most of our vocabulary seems either too specific or too vague to serve as an exact physical description. It is only sometimes, when the right image strikes, when some flukey piece of poetry occurs, that words succeed in capturing dance alive.

To photograph dance should be an easier task than writing about it, since photography deals in visual images, in recording the physical moment. Yet a really good dance photograph is as rare as a good piece of dance prose and is just as hampered by inbuilt limitations.

At a very basic level, the photographer is stuck with the fact that the photo is still, while dance moves, and that the photo is flat, while dance exists in three-dimensional space. He or she is also partly cursed by the photo's special reproductive accuracy – by the fact that it essentially shows us images of the real world, rather than those conjured out of the photographer's head.

This limits the opportunities for finding non-literal ways of recording the feeling of movement. Take the figures in Matisse's painting *The Dance* (1909-10). Their bodies do not remotely conform to normal human physiology, nor are they performing technical dance actions. Yet the sensuous exaggeration of their muscles, the intent curves of their bodies, the way as a group they press out to all four sides of the canvas, produce a wild kinetic energy and a powerful impression of thrust, gravity and rhythm.

Matisse's success in capturing movement is partly due to his distinctive line. But it is also facilitated by the fact that drawing and painting are themselves physically dynamic acts, so the trace of the painter's moving hand is recorded within the image. The photographer's ability to capture movement within a still image is far more laborious – far more the result of technological ingenuity than the natural by-product of the medium.

It is a more cumbersome business too setting up metaphors. In a famous lithograph of the 19th-century ballerina Marie Taglioni, the dancer is shown poised for flight on one toe, her weight scarcely bending the slender branch on which she perches. At a time when dancing on *pointe* was still a novelty, Taglioni's seemingly effortless and ethereal technique astounded her audiences, inspiring wild and extravagant claims for her other-worldly qualities. This simple pictorial fantasy not only captured the lightness and *ballon* of Taglioni's dancing, it also encapsulated the terms in which her fervent public perceived her.

Early dance photography was far more earth-bound, since the lengthy exposure time of each shot meant that dancers had to pose, they could not be shown mid-jump or in a split-second balance. Photographers could work through their own magic. In the early 20th century, Baron de Meyer's series of Nijinsky's *L'Après Midi d'un Faune* recreated the ballet's dreamy and mysterious atmosphere by means of soft-focus lenses, bounce light, gauze and much re-touching. And though he and other photographers could rarely capture the miracle of Nijinsky's jump, they *could* reproduce in detail the physique that produced it. In the Bert image of Nijinsky as *Le Dieu Bleu*, high-contrast light and shadow emphasise the heroic, muscular power of the dancer's legs, neck and chest, the solidity with which his weight thrust down through his foot, and the startling contrast of the exotic, almost androgynous beauty of his face. Nijinsky's ability to get deep under the skin of his roles is also captured here. The hieratic cast of the face, the flattened oriental position, the sculpted yet unconscious lines of the body make Nijinsky look like some true archaic deity rather than a 20th-century impersonation.

The intense theatricality of those Nijinsky photographs is equalled by some of the early images of Martha Graham. The high definition of Barbara Morgan's famous picture of Graham in *Letter to the World* creates a sense of movement both sculpted in its detail and vigorous in its action. The deep folds highlighted in Graham's skirt dramatise and amplify the powerful backward sweep of her leg, while the detail of her face thrusting towards the floor exaggerates the harrowing emotion of the moment with its long angular lines, heavily drooped eyelids and taut, elongated neck.

By the 50s and 60s, improved technology increasingly facilitated the snapping of dramatic split-second movement – a dancer floating at the zenith of a jump or poised on the vertiginous downward path of a fall. But if the positions which could be caught by the camera became more dramatic, they also became open to over-exposure. Out of context, one *grand jeté* could look pretty much like another,

Laurie Lewis, OPPOSITE: Darcey Bussell rehearsing her role in La Ronde, *choreographed for the Royal Ballet by Glen Tetley, and based on the Schnitzler play, a cyclical story of changing sexual partners set in Vienna. The production premièred in London in June 1993; OVERLEAF: Viviana Durante rehearsing her role in* La Ronde. *The movement was recorded on a single frame with a 20-second exposure. Both pictures were taken in the same photographic session.*

Chris Nash, The Cholmondeleys, Walky-Talky, *1992*

Chris Nash, Joseph Nadj, *Théâtre de la Bastille, Paris, 1989*

as countless dance calendars and coffee-table books testified.

Despite, perhaps because of new technology, dance photographers still have to use their eyes and their imaginations to construct the vivid, the memorable and the suggestive photo. Those who have to take their photographs in the dancers' time – at the theatre or in the rehearsal studio – have to read quickly and accurately. If the camera is capable of freezing the perfect moment, it's also capable of recording the imperfect moment. A pirouette that is photographed too soon is likely to show a fleetingly ungainly preparation of the foot, an unflatteringly transitional angle of the body, or a not quite in-position arm. In classical ballet it's easier for the photographer to tune into the shape and timing of a dance phrase. In modern or post-modern dance techniques, the startling image may be missed unless the photographer can intuit that the dancer is about to do something extraordinary. As Lois Greenfield has commented though, there is much less of a strict demarcation between the right and the wrong moment in these techniques, a much less circumscribed sense of what makes a great moment, as in her 1988 picture of Ashley Roland where it is not just the shape of the body but the flying tresses of hair that communicate the powerful downwards and backwards force of the movement. [see inside back cover]

That image was taken during an improvisation session that was specially set up, and photographers have far more control when they work in situations where they can dictate the light and the background, to some extent even the movement the dancers are doing. Many of Chris Nash's images achieve a dramatic clarity by virtue of their very deliberate composition – like his 1989 picture of the dancer Joseph Nadj. The bright white light at the back of the picture foregrounds Nadj as a dark, looming and powerful shape. The raised foot and knee pushing into the camera gives the viewer a pressing sense of the kicking dynamic of Nadj's leg movement, while his shadowed body and concealed face exaggerate the contracted downward force running through his torso. Nadj's movement is further amplified by the silhouetted swing of his coat and the echoing image of his shadow on the floor. And the chiaroscuro effect of the lighting injects a Hitchcockian tension into the image – we do not just look at Nadj, we wonder what role he is playing, what situation he finds himself in.

Nash's ability to suggest the plot or mood of the dance piece he is shooting is enriched by the distinctive special effects he creates – the way he splices images together, or adds words and drawings to create almost painterly metaphors and designs. In his photos of Lea Anderson's *Walky Talky* he eerily captures the dance's subject of bed times and nocturnal fantasies. One dancer dreams of a woman walking beneath a shadowed moon and reaching out for a giant lily, another lies sleeping with fish superimposed on her eyes, lips and hair.

In contrast to Nash's work, Laurie Lewis often tries to penetrate the private interior moments of dance. Many of his shots for *The Independent* newspaper show the dancers from the wings, from close up to the stage or in preparation for their roles, rather than actually dancing. Lewis also tries to capture the essence of a moving dancer rather than their frozen image, so in some of his pictures you see the dancer in a blur of light and action. Trace lines of the movement he or she has just been doing, and is just about to do, can be sensed alongside the actual movement being recorded – just as they can when one watches dance live. Lewis's shot of Laurie Booth improvising, for example, captures not only the rich and the ephemeral essence of a single dance moment, but also the totally evanescent nature of improvisation. It is an image that might satisfy Merce Cunningham himself.

ABOVE: Vaslav Nijinsky as the Blue God in Michel Fokine's ballet Le Dieu Bleu, *Ballets Russes, Théâtre du Chatelet, Paris, 13 May, 1912; LEFT: Barbara Morgan,* Martha Graham, Letter to the World, *1940. 'I studied her gesture, this floating forward: she's bowing to fate, but at the same time her flying leg shows the vitality that is going to carry her out of it . . . I didn't look upon it as the giving in to fate. I thought of it as a momentary giving in, with this brilliant after-flash.' Barbara Morgan*

THE PHENOMENOLOGY OF DANCE

by Dido Milne

Phenomenology is the pre-reflective search to describe ourselves and our world as we experience it. It describes the foundations of consciousness. The phenomenon of dance describes, therefore, the *immediate* encounter with the dance; the *lived* experience of the dance.

Maurice Merleau-Ponty, in *Phenomenology of Perception,* explores how our bodies are the way we *are* in the world, and in moving them how we reach out and communicate with the world. Our bodies are not 'objective entities' but '*lived* totalities'. He speaks of syn-esthesis, a combination of the visual and the aural, making it possible to '*see* sound' and '*hear* sight'. Stravinsky, who composed many works for George Balanchine, refers to this when he says, 'To see Balanchine's choreography of the movements is to hear the music with one's own eyes . . . The dance emphasises relationships of which I had hardly been aware.' [1] The senses work in unison to create a very rich experience, and it is often difficult to gauge the contribution from any one sense in such an experience. In clenching our fists, we experience a strong tactile sensation, yet equally we have a vivid image of what we look like at that moment, without actually seeing ourselves. Dancers, in particular, have a heightened awareness of their body contours when in motion.

Dance has long suffered intellectual neglect because of the low status given to the human body. Mind-body dualists argued that the mind was the essence of the human being, and the body was relegated to the role of a vehicle to house and transport the mind. Dance, as a body art, was seen as irrational, subjective, to do merely with the expression of the dancer's emotions, as opposed to an art that could be analysed in an objective way. Yet phenomenologists have shown how the lived body *is* the means through which we essentially understand what it is to be human. Therefore dance, which explores all the complexities of the body, does merit investigation.

One of the major challenges of modern dance has been to balance the weight given to visual perception against that given to the other senses. In 1924, Ortega y Gasset published *The Dehumanisation of Art,* one of the first major essays on the modernist tendency towards abstraction and self-purification. He believed that the goal of art was to create an environment of perception in which the act of seeing was unclouded by feeling. 'Aesthetic pleasure must be a seeing pleasure . . . and seeing requires distance.' [2] Balanchine, likewise, strove to obtain a perception of objective purity. The best seat in the house for a Balanchine ballet is plumb centre, half way back, from where the complex symmetry of the piece can be fully appreciated. He wished to 'free' the mind in order to see the dancing. In his ballets an impersonal style is achieved by the dancers dissolving their individuality in the vision of the maestro.

The traditional proscenium arch, which establishes a critical distance to view the dance through a frame, emphasises the optical way in which the work is to be viewed, similar to the way one would view a painting. Perspective privileges the viewer, dividing the voyeur on one side of the screen from the object under scrutiny on the other. It allows the object to be drawn and measured, thus known and understood. The process is seen as a highly rational, objective means of ordering and representing the world. More recently, however, perspective has been exposed as a highly artificial construct, since visually we perceive the world through a pair of moving eyes and not through a single stationary viewpoint. Proximity to the world of objects dissolves the objectivity of any one standpoint that exists in perspective. In contemporary dance, the dancer is 'in-the-midst' of the external world of space and objects. The living body of the dancer is in continuous intimate contact with this world. Initially, this closeness can seem to reduce the clarity and order in the dance, but I would suggest that it can lead to a deeper understanding of the art form; in the long term, maybe, a more objective understanding.

More avant-garde theatre design dismantles the traditional voyeuristic relationship between spectator and dancer. In recent designs the auditorium is linked in a far more immediate way to the stage, enabling the audience to feel the lived experience of the dance. The degree of immediate, felt force, flowing between spectator and dancer, differs greatly among choreographers. In the work of many post-modern choreographers, the primitive inspiration gives the dance a strong tactile sensation. A movement such as a contraction derived from the basic rhythm of breathing, is designed to radiate out to the audience, then back to the dancer, creating a strong sympathetic response in the musculature of the onlooker. Balanchine avoided these movements precisely because they removed the reflective distance that he sought.

We tend to view fine art through this critical distance, with the frame directing the focus of the eye. Yet in the creation of the work this distance is usually absent. The process itself is far more tactile. For example, in life drawing, when artists attempt to capture a particular pose, they may trace the prevalent line of force which runs through the body of the model they are observing, by first tracing the gesture in the air with a sweep of the arm, and later by a gesture made with the whole body. This ensures that the first critical line applied to paper captures the dynamism of the body in front of them.

The distinction between touching and looking at an object is that the latter represents both a physical and a mental step away from the experience. Erwin Straus, the German psychologist, notes that the ego, or 'I', of a person in everyday life (realm of purposeful movement) is situated at the base of the nose between the eyes. When addressing someone, this is where you focus. In this realm we move with reference to a fixed point, an immovable *here*, which gives all our movements a direction; it is the world of optically structured space. In dance, however, Straus observes that the 'I' moves to the region of the trunk. The 'I', situated in the dancer's torso, results in the 'direction' moving or turning with the dancer herself. Thus dance is not related to any one direction. The motor activity has its own momentum.

Following his 'lived through' description of dance, Straus emphasises the link between dance and music. He questions whether spatiality alters in the different spheres of sensory experience. Would an optical spatiality differ from an acoustical one? Are there different forms of motor activity and perception that correspond to them? 'Tones approach us, come to us, and surrounding us, drift on; they fill space, shaping themselves in temporal sequences.'[3] He contrasts this remarkable relationship between tone and time with the characteristics of optical spatiality. Colours are the mark of an object, appearing in a precise direction relative to ourselves, even if we misjudge their true distance. (Yellow as it inclines towards white tends to advance towards the eye, whereas blue as it inclines towards black does the converse.) We can, however, always point to colours as being 'over there'; they demarcate space for us. Tone on the contrary unifies space, separating itself from the sound source, which allows it to have an autonomous existence. It fills the air, enveloping us in its midst, and in this way it is non-directional, free to roam like the dance. For when the 'I' is situated in the torso, it creates the kind of movement that allows freedom in the space, so the dancer can expand or contract his or her body space at will.

Dance is a unified temporal and spatial entity, 'a perpetually moving form whose "moments" are all of a piece.'[4] This understanding of dance questions how it should be staged. The space of dance is unbounded, non-directional, homogeneous. Therefore, the traditional proscenium arch seems an arbitrary way to frame the performance. Straus reminds us of our familiar feelings of alienation and removal when watching a film with no sound, and how we are immediately drawn into the picture when the soundtrack is re-introduced, even if the music is somehow not very appropriate. 'Space filled with sound is enough to establish a connection between viewer and picture.'[5] Tone bridges boundaries connecting the dancer's movements with the audience. As it envelops the auditorium an indivisible whole is created, which speaks of the dance. When watching dance, 'we do not see separate objective factors with no unifying centre. What we see is something that perhaps can only be empirically written as forcetimespace; an indivisible wholeness appears before us.'[6]

Notes

1 B Taper, *Balanchine, A Biography*, 1987, University of California Press, pp258-59.

2 Ortega y Gasset, *The Dehumanisation of Art*, New York Times, 1924.

3 E Straus, *Phenomenological Psychology*, 1966, Tavistock Publications, London, p7.

4 M Sheets-Johnstone, *The Phenomenology of Dance*, 1966, Tavistock Publications, p22.

5 E Straus, *op cit*, p20.

6 M Sheets-Johnstone, *op cit*, p14.

Jean Cocteau,
Igor Stravinsky, *1913,*
pen and ink

Ashley Roland, 1990

LOIS GREENFIELD

LIBERATING THE DANCER FROM THE DANCE
by William A Ewing

At a gala performance in September 1992, celebrating Lois Greenfield's retrospective exhibition at New York's International Center of Photography, David Pàrsons electrified the audience with his solo, *Caught*, in which he dances in darkness, lit at rapid intervals with a strobe triggered by the dancer himself, but only when he is in the air. The effect is breathtaking, as if Parsons is in continual flight, soaring, gliding, hovering over the heads of the audience. And because the strobe is so fast (measured in thousandths of a second), the effect is one of seeing a rapid succession of still – *absolutely* still – images, like an animated Muybridge.

I had asked for *Caught* to be performed on this occasion as the *pièce de résistance* in an evening of dance by Parsons, Daniel Ezralow, Ashley Roland, Bill T Jones, Elizabeth Streb, and others who had worked with Greenfield over the years. The choice of *Caught* was not only a matter of a dance that *looked* like dance photography – by implication, Greenfield's photography – but a dance that had been wholly inspired *by* dance photography – again, Greenfield's. For the first time, I believe, the traditional roles of dance and photography had been inverted. No longer was dance the uncontested leader, photography the follower; no longer was photography merely the handmaiden of the dance, there to perform the functions of documentation and/or idealisation. The partnership of dance and photography was finally placed on an equal footing. As such, *Caught* was the perfect tribute to Greenfield's art, which has always insisted on her medium being accorded equal respect with its subject matter.

While Greenfield professes great respect for the dance, and is immensely knowledgeable in the modern and post-modern area (having been the *Village Voice* dance photographer for 20 years), her loyalty is first and foremost to the photographic image. Since the 19th century much wishful thinking has been voiced about dance photography's ability to 'capture' the dance, but Greenfield recognised from the outset that this was fundamentally impossible. The image does not, cannot, simulate the dance; it has no music, no ambient sounds of footwork, no peripheral vision, and most significantly, no movement – only fractured time and fragmented space. It can represent the dance, or evoke it, but it cannot preserve it. The split-second image is a universe unto itself, standing or falling according to its own dynamics – pictorial dynamics, not dance dynamics. Early on, Greenfield understood that a great dance or a great dancer does not automatically translate into a great photographic image; conversely, a skilful photographer can make a spectacular photograph with a mediocre dance. The photograph is not a slice of reality – it is an illusion. The general audience for dance photographs is, of course, obsessed with celebrity, and virtually any image reasonably in focus of, say, a Baryshnikov or Nureyev, will become an object of veneration, even a fetish. Lucrative careers have been built on this premise, but at a price: few dance photographers have been acknowledged as important photographers *per se*, and justifiably included in histories of fine art photography. Greenfield's allegiance to the photographic image qualifies her as an exception to this historically lacklustre state of affairs.

This does not mean that an uncompromising photographer cannot be of service to the dance. Think in terms of two 'Lois Greenfields': first, a professional dance photographer who *does* provide dance companies, dancers and choreographers with iconic images – sometimes depicting/interpreting specific dances or dancers, at other times providing 'generic' imagery of choreography (for example, a Merce Cunningham image she made in 1992 was used as a company 'logo' throughout the following season). This was the Greenfield who had gravitated to the dance in the early 1970s as a consequence of her photo-journalism, and recognised a market and a livelihood. The dance world has long admired and respected this competent and creative interpreter, whose vision has become a feature of the New York dance scene through company brochures, posters, and most importantly, the pages of New York's *Village Voice*, where week after week her images complement critic Deborah Jowitt's reports. What is not adequately appreciated, however, is the degree of creative involvement in the process, for what is seen on the printed page often exists only in the form of a photographic image. The specific movements and gestures, choreographed by the photographer for the camera, are not present in the staged performance; they have their counterparts in performance, but they are unique to the photograph. That the dancers and choreographers are satisfied, often delighted, with the results testifies to her grasp of the spirit of a particular dance, even while she takes extensive

ABOVE: Morleigh Steinberg, Ashley Roland, Jamey Hampton and Daniel Ezralow, ISO Dance Company, 1987;
OPPOSITE: Arthur Aviles, 1993

Henry Beer, Paula Gifford, Peter Larose, Elizabeth Streb and Jorge Collazo, Elizabeth Streb/Ringside Inc, 1988

liberties with 'the letter'.

The second Greenfield is, in a sense, not a dance photographer at all, but an image maker obsessed with the human body in motion, much as Eadweard Muybridge was 100 years ago. For this Lois Greenfield, dancers are important, first, because their movements can be controlled with great precision (so that she can ask Dancer X to land on one precise point while Dancer Y lands on another); second, because the dancers' abilities to jump, twist, re-form themselves, and so on, are far greater than those of ordinary mortals. But if Greenfield relies on the active, enthusiastic collaboration of her dancers, she never relinquishes her direction and control. This is the meaning behind Greenfield's enigmatic statement, 'I tell the dancers to leave their choreography at the door.' While depending upon their exceptional skills and talents, she dispenses with their preconceived ideas about how they are expected to perform. Instead, emphasis is placed on the element of play and free association. Consequently, the sessions are often exhilarating for the dancers. Says Greenfield, quite justifiably, 'I liberate the dancer from the dance.'

The results of her freewheeling approach speak for themselves. Often the process yields the unexpected – a chance convergence of limbs, for example, or an illusion of utter stillness where there had been violent motion. While fun for both dancer and photographer on one level, the process is demanding – physically and intellectually. Movements are repeated over and over with minor variations, until something begins to emerge. In-process Polaroids (ie, instant photographs) are studied by both parties, suggestions are made and then explored, until Greenfield is satisfied that she has broken through to the heart of the matter. All of this activity transpires in a surprisingly small space, some 12 feet wide by 15 feet deep, the width dictated by the maximum dimensions of photographic background paper. To the bystander the process appears as absolute chaos, too fast for any or pattern to be discerned. What appears in the final image as, say, a serene and effortless flight is in fact a physically violent act, with the dancer crashing to the ground or hurtling off the set into a wall; only their training and peak conditions prevent injury. The bystander may also be astonished to learn that the photographer not only sees the scene in the viewfinder upside down, but left to right, so that a dancer hurtling across the stage from one direction appears in the viewfinder to be coming from the other. Choosing the right moment ('moment' being a misnomer, if ever there was one, as the image is made in a fraction of a second) presupposes anticipating it, as to wait for it would be to miss it.

Greenfield liberates her dancers from more than the dance – she frees them from the constraints of time and space as well, even in a sense from their own bodies. As Parsons hung and hovered in *Caught*, he and his friends soar, plummet, float and bounce in the camera's eye, oblivious to the constraints of gravity and the supposed limitations of their own anatomy. Greenfield's square frame, or framed 'box', is a magical place where childhood fantasies can be recovered and indulged. In fact, the black bars which enclose a Greenfield image delineate the limits of the negative, but they function on a literal level as well, constraining and compressing the dancers while hinting at the world beyond.

But this box, this cage, is not without means of escape; the dancers may play within the cage, seemingly hang on the 'bars' or career off them, but they may also slip between them and escape . . . In the series of images which gave the name to Greenfield's new book, *Breaking Bounds*,[1] this idea was explored in a series of images in which Parsons danced around and through a wood frame which Greenfield had had constructed – the figurative frame of the negative border made real. For anyone familiar with the choreography of Elizabeth Streb, with whom Greenfield feels a strong affinity, this series may be recognised as an analogue; Streb has had her dancers physically constrained in just such a real box.

Sometimes the Greenfield frame feels confining, but at other times the space inside seems unspeakably vast. It's the way in which the figures are juxtaposed, or placed on different planes, or the ways in which they are made to connect, that determines this scale. Less remarked upon by her critics, but no less effective, is Greenfield's use of negative space. It is more of an ether than a void, a magical element unique to a Greenfield image. Of late she has had her imitators but this particular element has exceeded their reach.

It is tension, or rather tensions, between various opposing forces which empower a Greenfield image; between the force of gravity and weightlessness; between the linear and the curvilinear; between attraction and repulsion; between vertical, diagonal, and horizontal vectors; between serenity of expression and taxing physical activity; between balance and imbalance; between freedom and constraint; between connection and disconnection; between figuration and abstraction; and between order and chaos.

But ultimately, what fascinates and confounds Greenfield's viewer is the paradox: the illusion of movement in a still image. The paradox, of course, is as old as photography itself, but never before has it been so artfully resolved. Greenfield has located a territory of her own, the fine line between the body at rest and the body in motion.

Note

1 *Breaking Bounds* by William A Ewing is published by Thames & Hudson.

Janet Lilly, Bill T Jones and Heidi Latsky in Chatter, *Bill T Jones/Arnie Zane & Company, 1988*